KETCHUP VOCA

LEVEL 1 1

i-Scream edu

영어 공부의 핵심은 단어입니다.

케찹보카로
영어 단어 실력을 키우고,
상위 1% 어휘력을
따라잡아 보세요!

케찹보카
친구들

만화 스토리
친구들의 좌충우돌 일상이 그려진
재미있는 만화를 보며
단어 뜻을 배우고,
문장에 어떻게 활용되는지
알아볼 수 있어요!

Dennis	엉뚱하고 낙천적인 성격의 자유로운 영혼! 예측 불가에, 공부에도 관심이 없지만, 운이 좋아 뭘 해도 잘 풀린대요.	
Rod	인내심이 크고 생각도 깊은, 다정다감 엄친아! 개구쟁이 쌍둥이 누나, 애완묘 루나가 있어 혼자 있는 것보단 함께 하는 것을 좋아해요.	
Kiara	노래를 좋아하는 사교성의 아이콘! 솔직하고 모든 일에 적극적이지만, 금방 사랑에 빠지는 짝사랑 전문가래요.	
Sally	논리적이고 긍정적인 모범생! 친구들과 장난도 많이 치지만, 호기심이 많아 관심 분야에 다양한 지식을 갖고 있어요.	
Mong	친구들이 궁금한 것이 있을 때 나타나는 해결사! 너무 아는 것이 많아서 어느 별에서 왔는지 궁금하기도 해요.	

Know   Exercise   Think   Check   Habit

KETCH UP

망각 제로 단어 기억하기 습관으로
기억 장기화

게임으로 즐겁게 리뷰하고 테스트로 더블 체크

만화 스토리 〉단어 〉문장 순으로
단어 의미를 이해하며 모국어처럼 습득

이미지 연상 쓰기 연습으로 실제 단어 활용, 적용

주제별로 초등 필수＆고난도 단어 학습하며
상위 1% 단어 마스터

KETCH UP
Makes you Catch up.

체계적인 4 Steps 시스템으로 학습 완성!

Step 1	Step 2	Step 3	Step 4

Day 1~4

Day 5

Step 1

Warm up 망각 제로 & 스토리 단어 이해로 학습 준비하기

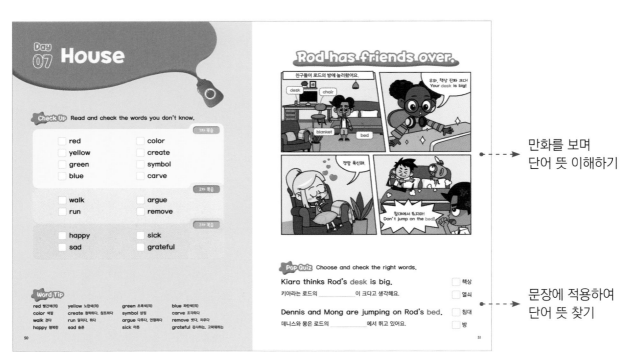

만화를 보며
단어 뜻 이해하기

문장에 적용하여
단어 뜻 찾기

※ 망각 제로는 p10에서 확인하세요!

Catch up 듣고, 말하고, 읽고, 쓰며, 상위 1% 단어 따라잡기

QR 찍어 단어 듣고 따라 말하기 ▶ 케챱병을 색칠하며 3번 반복하기

Basic Words 초등 필수 단어

Jump Up Words 고난도 단어

품사 기호

v	verb (동사)	**adv**	adverb (부사)	**conj**	conjunction (접속사)
n	noun (명사)	**prep**	preposition (전치사)	**pron**	pronoun (대명사)
a	adjective (형용사)	**det**	determiner (한정사)	**num**	numeral (수사)

케찹보카와 함께
상위 1% CATCH UP!

Step 3

Skill up 두뇌 자극 이미지 연상 학습으로 실력 강화하기

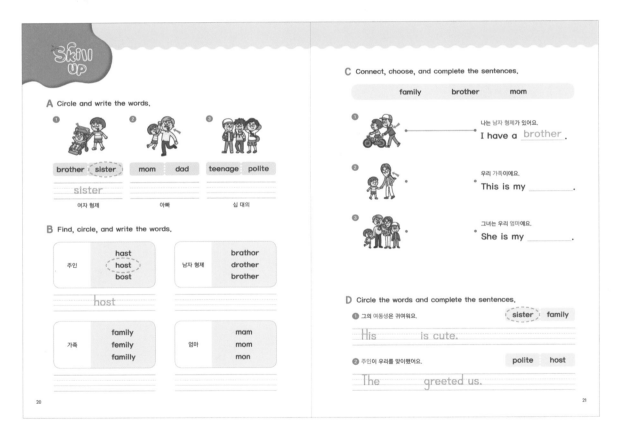

유형 1	유형 2	유형 3	유형 4
이미지 연상을 통해 단어 완성하기	우리말에 맞춰 스펠링 배열하여 단어 쓰기	이미지와 문장을 연결하여 단어 뜻 이해하기	배운 단어 적용하여 문장 완성하여 쓰기

Wrap up 게임과 최종 평가를 통해 단어 학습 마무리하기

쉬어가기

다양한 유형의 재미있는 게임하며 단어 복습하기!

Word Maze	Word Coloring	Word Puzzle	Word Search
알맞은 스펠링으로 이뤄진 단어를 따라가 미로 찾기	알맞은 단어를 색칠하며, 배운 단어 기억하기	주어진 문장에 알맞은 단어를 쓰며 퍼즐 완성하기	다양한 알파벳 속 배운 단어를 찾아 쓰기 연습하기

복습&테스트

지금까지 배운 단어 정리하고, 테스트로 최종 점검!
뜯어서 쓰는 나만의 단어장까지!

Study Planner & Contents

Part I

FINISH

START

Day 01 Feelings

※ 망각 제로는 [DAY 02]부터 시작합니다.

망각 제로란?

망각 제로는
학습 주기를 활용해서 복습하는 거야.

지난번에 공부했던 단어 중에
아는 것과 모르는 것을 확인해 볼 수 있겠네!

Day 07 House

Check Up Read and check the words you don't know.

1차 복습

- [ ] red
- [ ] yellow
- [ ] green
- [ ] blue

- [ ] color
- [ ] create
- [ ] symbol
- [ ] carve

2차 복습

- [ ] walk
- [ ] run

- [ ] argue
- [ ] remove

3차 복습

- [ ] happy
- [ ] sad

- [ ] sick
- [ ] grateful

Word Tip

red 빨간(색)의   yellow 노란색(의)   green 초록색의   blue 파란색의
create 창조하다, 창조하다   symbol 상징   carve 조각하다
run 달리다, 뛰다   argue 다투다, 언쟁하다   remove 벗다, 지우다
grateful 감사하는, 고마워하는

Pop Quiz Choose and check the right words.

Kiara thinks Rod's desk is big.
키아라는 로드의 _____ 이 크다고 생각해요.
- [ ] 책상
- [ ] 열쇠

Dennis and Mong are jumping on Rod's bed.
데니스와 몽은 로드의 _____ 에서 뛰고 있어요.
- [ ] 침대
- [ ] 방

51

Check Up

복습 주기에 맞춰 반복 학습하기

1차 복습	1일 전 공부한 단어
2차 복습	3일 전 공부한 단어
3차 복습	7일 전 공부한 단어

Word Tip

정확한 단어 뜻 확인하기

" 우리 같이
망각 제로 학습해 보자 "

Rod looks so sad.

Pop Quiz Choose and check the right words.

Rod looks sad.

로드는 _____ 보여요.

☐ 행복한

☑ 슬픈

Rod is afraid of going bald.

로드는 대머리가 될까 봐 _____요.

☐ 두려워하는

☐ 화가 난

 Write the **Basic Words** and **Jump Up Words**.

happy 행복한	**I am** happy.  나는 행복해요. happy

sad 슬픈	**He looks** sad.  그는 슬퍼 보여요.

angry 화가 난	**We are** angry.  우리는 화가 나요.

afraid
두려워하는

He is afraid of spiders. ⓐ

그는 거미를 두려워해요.

_____
- -
_____

sick
아픈

She is sick. ⓐ

그녀는 아파요.

_____
- -
_____

anxious
불안해하는,
걱정하는

I was anxious. ⓐ

나는 불안했어요.

_____
- -
_____

grateful
감사하는,
고마워하는

I am grateful for your help. ⓐ

도와주셔서 감사해요.

_____
- -
_____

bold
대담한

She is a bold woman. ⓐ

그녀는 대담한 여성이에요.

_____
- -
_____

A Circle the letters and complete the words.

1

(p) (a) e q

h a p p y

행복한

2

c b s z

_ i _ k

아픈

3

g t r u

a n _ _ y

화가 난

B Unscramble and write the words.

1 불안해하는, 걱정하는

o n i u x s a

anxious

2 두려워하는

d a r f a i

3 대담한

b l o d

4 감사하는, 고마워하는

g t f r e a u l

C Connect and fill in the blanks.

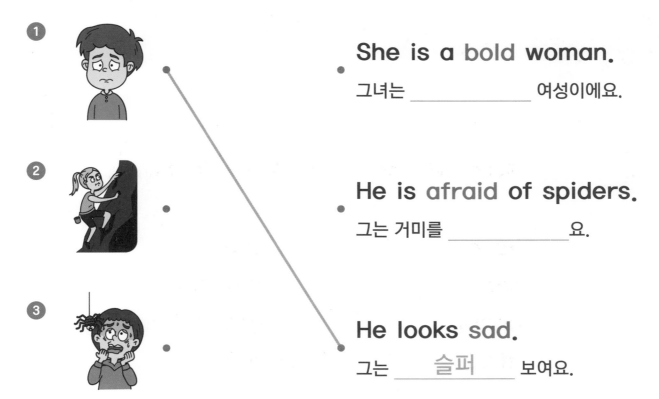

1

2

3

She is a bold woman.

그녀는 _____ 여성이에요.

He is afraid of spiders.

그는 거미를 _____요.

He looks sad.

그는 ___슬퍼___ 보여요.

D Choose and complete the sentences.

grateful	anxious	angry

1 우리는 화가 나요.

We are ___angry___.

2 도와주셔서 감사해요.

I am _____ for your help.

3 나는 불안했어요.

I was _____.

Day 02 Family

Check Up Read and check the words you don't know.

1차 복습

- [ ] happy
- [ ] sad
- [ ] angry
- [ ] afraid
- [ ] sick
- [ ] anxious
- [ ] grateful
- [ ] bold

※ **망각 제로!** 1일 전 학습한 단어를 복습해요.

 **Word Tip**

happy 행복한   **sad** 슬픈   **angry** 화가 난   **afraid** 두려워하는
sick 아픈   **anxious** 불안해하는, 걱정하는   **grateful** 감사하는, 고마워하는   **bold** 대담한

Meet Dennis's family.

Pop Quiz Choose and check the right words.

Dennis has a baby sister.

데니스는 _____이 있어요.

☐ 남동생

☐ 여동생

Sally wants to have an older brother.

샐리는 _____를 갖고 싶어해요.

☐ 오빠

☐ 언니

Listen & Say Listen, say, and color.

Read & Write Write the **Basic Words** and **Jump Up Words**.

family 가족	**This is my family.** 우리 가족이에요. _____ _____ _____	 n

dad 아빠	**He is my dad.** 그는 우리 아빠예요. _____ _____ _____	n

mom 엄마	**She is my mom.** 그녀는 우리 엄마예요. _____ _____ _____	 n

brother
남자 형제
(형, 오빠, 남동생)

I have a brother. (n)

나는 남자 형제가 있어요.

_____

_____

_____

sister
여자 형제
(누나, 언니, 여동생)

His sister is cute. (n)

그의 여동생은 귀여워요.

_____

_____

_____

teenage
십 대의

They are teenage boys. (a)

그들은 십 대 남자아이들이에요.

_____

_____

_____

host
주인, 주최하다

The host greeted us. (n) (v)

주인이 우리를 맞이했어요.

_____

_____

_____

polite
공손한

She is polite. (a)

그녀는 공손해요.

_____

_____

_____

A Circle and write the words.

1 **2** **3**

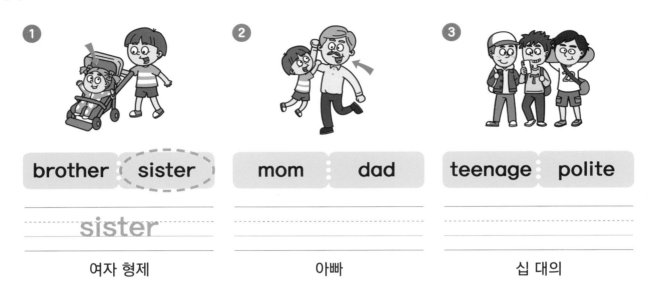

| brother | (sister) | | mom | dad | | teenage | polite |

sister

여자 형제   아빠   십 대의

B Find, circle, and write the words.

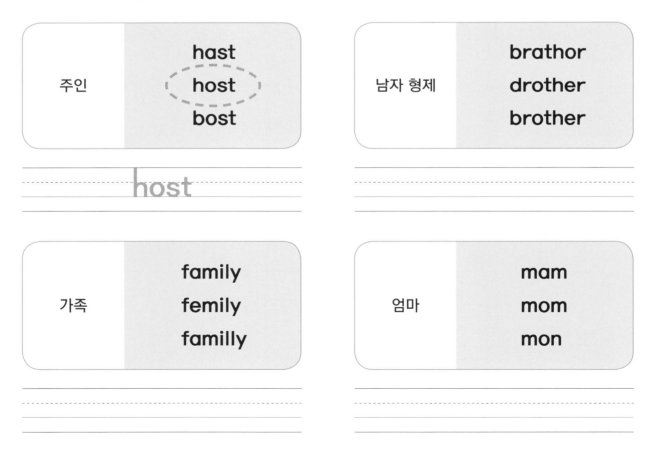

| 주인 | hast / (host) / bost |
| 남자 형제 | brathor / drother / brother |

host

| 가족 | family / femily / familly |
| 엄마 | mam / mom / mon |

C Connect, choose, and complete the sentences.

family	brother	mom

1 나는 남자 형제가 있어요.

I have a ___brother___ .

2 우리 가족이에요.

This is my _____ .

3 그녀는 우리 엄마예요.

She is my _____ .

D Circle the words and complete the sentences.

1 그의 여동생은 귀여워요.

(sister) family

His _____ is cute.

2 주인이 우리를 맞이했어요.

polite host

The _____ greeted us.

Day 03 Animals

Check Up Read and check the words you don't know.

1차 복습

☐ family   ☐ sister

☐ dad   ☐ teenage

☐ mom   ☐ host

☐ brother   ☐ polite

※ **망각 제로!** 1일 전 학습한 단어를 복습해요.

Word Tip

family 가족   **dad** 아빠   **mom** 엄마   **brother** 남자 형제

sister 여자 형제   **teenage** 십 대의   **host** 주인, 주최하다   **polite** 공손한

What animals do you like?

Pop Quiz Choose and check the right words.

Kiara likes cats.

키아라는 _____를 좋아해요.

☐ 강아지
☐ 고양이

Sally thinks ducks are so cute.

샐리는 _____가 아주 귀엽다고 생각해요.

☐ 오리
☐ 새

Listen & Say   Listen, say, and color.

Read & Write   Write the **Basic Words** and **Jump Up Words**.

bird 새	**There is a bird on the grass.** 잔디 위에 새가 있어요. _____ - - - - - - - - - - - - - - _____

cat 고양이	**The cat is cute.** 그 고양이는 귀여워요. _____ - - - - - - - - - - - - - - _____

dog 개	**The dog has a bone.** 개가 뼈다귀를 가지고 있어요. _____ - - - - - - - - - - - - - - _____

duck
오리

The duck started quacking.
오리가 꽥꽥거리기 시작했어요.

n

_____
- -
_____

horse
말

I rode a horse.
나는 말을 탔어요.

n

_____
- -
_____

enemy
적

They attacked the enemy.
그들은 적을 공격했어요.

n

_____
- -
_____

follow
따라가다

My dogs always follow me.
내 개들은 항상 나를 따라다녀요.

v

_____
- -
_____

various
다양한,
여러 가지의

There are various animals.
다양한 동물들이 있어요.

a

_____
- -
_____

A Circle and trace the words.

1

새	고양이

bird

2

개	말

dog

3

고양이	오리

duck

B Connect and write the words.

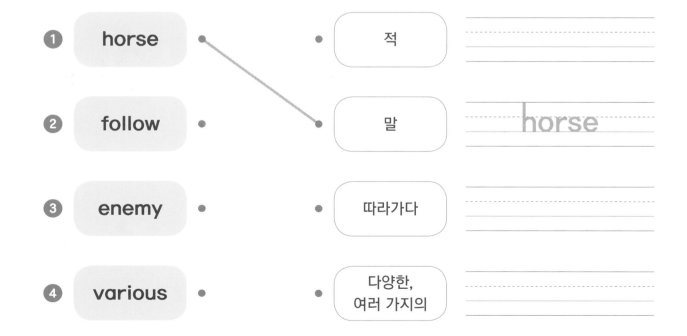

1 horse • • 적

2 follow • • 말   horse

3 enemy • • 따라가다

4 various • • 다양한, 여러 가지의

C Connect and fill in the blanks.

1

My dogs always follow me.

내 개들은 항상 나를 _____.

2

There are various animals.

_____ 동물들이 있어요.

3

I rode a horse.

나는 _____을 탔어요.

D Choose and complete the sentences.

enemy	cat	bird

1 그 고양이는 귀여워요.

The _____ is cute.

2 잔디 위에 새가 있어요.

There is a _____ on the grass.

3 그들은 적을 공격했어요.

They attacked the _____.

Day 04 Actions

1차 복습

- [ ] bird
- [ ] cat
- [ ] dog
- [ ] duck
- [ ] horse
- [ ] enemy
- [ ] follow
- [ ] various

2차 복습

- [ ] happy
- [ ] sad
- [ ] angry
- [ ] afraid

※ **망각 제로!** 1일 전 3일 전 학습한 단어를 복습해요.

Word Tip

bird 새	**cat** 고양이	**dog** 개	**duck** 오리
horse 말	**enemy** 적	**follow** 따라가다	**various** 다양한, 여러 가지의
happy 행복한	**sad** 슬픈	**angry** 화가 난	**afraid** 두려워하는

Let's walk together.

PoP Quiz Choose and check the right words.

Rod walks in the park every day.

로드는 매일 공원을 _____.

☐ 걷다

☐ 춤추다

Rod saw Dennis running toward him.

로드는 데니스가 자신을 향해 _____ 것을 보았어요.

☐ 노래하다

☐ 달리다, 뛰다

Read & Write Write the **Basic Words** and **Jump Up Words**.

walk 걷다	**I walk to school.** 나는 학교에 걸어가요.

run 달리다, 뛰다	**He runs fast.** 그는 빠르게 달려요.

call 부르다, 전화하다	**I called her name.** 나는 그녀의 이름을 불렀어요.

sing
노래하다

They like to sing.
그들은 노래하는 것을 좋아해요.

_____

dance
춤추다

He dances with his mom.
그는 엄마와 춤춰요.

_____

argue
다투다, 언쟁하다

I argued with my friend.
나는 친구와 다퉜어요.

_____

remove
벗다, 치우다

Dad removes his jacket.
아빠가 재킷을 벗어요.

_____

frown
눈살을 찌푸리다

She frowned at him.
그녀는 그를 보고 눈살을 찌푸렸어요.

_____

A Circle the letters and complete the words.

① a u e i

r _ n

달리다, 뛰다

② a b z g

_ r u e

다투다, 언쟁하다

③ f g r u

_ o w n

눈살을 찌푸리다

B Unscramble and write the words.

① 걷다   a k l w   ....

② 부르다, 전화하다   l a c l   ....

③ 춤추다   e d a c n   ....

④ 벗다, 치우다   e r v o e m   ....

C Connect, choose, and complete the sentences.

walk	sing	dances

1 그들은 노래하는 것을 좋아해요.

They like to _____.

2 나는 학교에 걸어가요.

I _____ to school.

3 그는 엄마와 춤춰요.

He _____ with his mom.

D Circle the words and complete the sentences.

1 나는 친구와 다퉜어요.

argued   frowned

I _____ with my friend.

2 아빠가 재킷을 벗어요.

runs   removes

Dad _____ his jacket.

Body Parts

Check Up Read and check the words you don't know.

1차 복습

☐ walk	☐ dance
☐ run	☐ argue
☐ call	☐ remove
☐ sing	☐ frown

2차 복습

☐ family	☐ dad
☐ mom	☐ teenage

※ 망각 제로! 1일 전 3일 전 학습한 단어를 복습해요.

 **Word Tip**

walk 걷다   **run** 달리다, 뛰다   **call** 부르다, 전화하다   **sing** 노래하다

dance 춤추다   **argue** 다투다, 언쟁하다   **remove** 벗다, 치우다   **frown** 눈살을 찌푸리다

family 가족   **mom** 엄마   **dad** 아빠   **teenage** 십 대의

I like my face.

Rod likes his nose.

로드는 그의 _____를 마음에 들어 해요.

- [ ] 코
- [ ] 입

Sally has beautiful eyes.

샐리는 아름다운 _____을 가지고 있어요.

- [ ] 귀
- [ ] 눈

35

 **Listen, say, and color.**

Read & Write **Write the Basic Words and Jump Up Words.**

face 얼굴	**Look at my face.** n 내 얼굴을 보세요.

eye 눈	**I have two eyes.** n 나는 눈이 두 개예요.

nose 코	**He has a big nose.** n 그는 큰 코를 가지고 있어요.

36

mouth
입

I opened my mouth.

나는 입을 벌렸어요.

n

ear
귀

A rabbit has long ears.

토끼는 긴 귀를 가지고 있어요.

n

nervous
불안해하는

I was so nervous my mouth was dry.

나는 너무 불안해서 입이 바싹 말랐어요.

a

protect
보호하다, 지키다

Sunglasses protect my eyes.

선글라스는 내 눈을 보호해요.

v

bare
맨, 벌거벗은

I touched it with my bare hands.

나는 그것을 맨손으로 만졌어요.

a

Skill Up

A Circle and write the words.

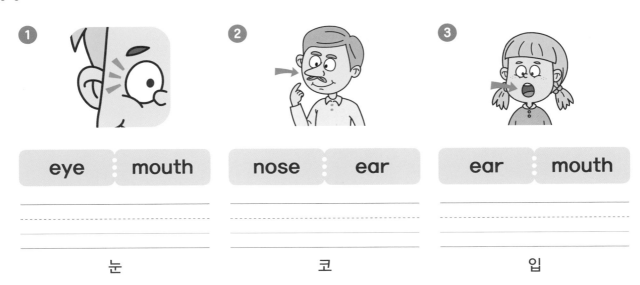

1

eye	mouth

_____

눈

2

nose	ear

_____

코

3

ear	mouth

_____

입

B Find, circle, and write the words.

얼굴	face fase feec

_____

맨, 벌거벗은	bere bare brae

_____

보호하다, 지키다	plotate protact protect

_____

불안해하는	nurvous nervous nerveus

_____

C Connect and fill in the blanks.

1

Look at my face.

내 _____을 보세요.

2

A rabbit has long ears.

토끼는 긴 _____를 가지고 있어요.

3

Sunglasses protect my eyes.

선글라스는 내 눈을 _____.

D Choose and complete the sentences.

mouth	nose	bare

1 그는 큰 코를 가지고 있어요.

He has a big _____.

2 나는 입을 벌렸어요.

I opened my _____.

3 나는 그것을 맨손으로 만졌어요.

I touched it with my _____ hands.

WORD MAZE Follow the correctly spelled words.

START

happy

mom

muoth

cat

mouth

sad

walk

dad

biird

bird

mouce

mouse

noce

eye

eie

dog

ear

rne

run

FINISH

40

happy 행복한	**sad** 슬픈	**angry** 화가 난	**afraid** 두려워하는	**sick** 아픈
anxious 불안해하는, 걱정하는	**grateful** 감사하는, 고마워하는	**bold** 대담한	**family** 가족	**dad** 아빠
mom 엄마	**brother** 남자 형제	**sister** 여자 형제	**teenage** 십 대의	**host** 주인, 주최하다
polite 공손한	**bird** 새	**cat** 고양이	**dog** 개	**duck** 오리
horse 말	**enemy** 적	**follow** 따라가다	**various** 다양한, 여러 가지의	**walk** 걷다
run 달리다, 뛰다	**call** 부르다, 전화하다	**sing** 노래하다	**dance** 춤추다	**argue** 다투다, 언쟁하다
remove 벗다, 치우다	**frown** 눈살을 찌푸리다	**face** 얼굴	**eye** 눈	**nose** 코
mouth 입	**ear** 귀	**nervous** 불안해하는	**protect** 보호하다, 지키다	**bare** 맨, 벌거벗은

맞힌 개수 : ☐ / 40

❶ angry		㉑ 행복한	
❷ afraid		㉒ 슬픈	
❸ anxious		㉓ 아픈	
❹ grateful		㉔ 대담한	
❺ brother		㉕ 가족	
❻ sister		㉖ 아빠	
❼ teenage		㉗ 엄마	
❽ polite		㉘ 주인, 주최하다	
❾ horse		㉙ 춤추다	
❿ enemy		㉚ 노래하다	
⓫ follow		㉛ 새	
⓬ various		㉜ 고양이	
⓭ argue		㉝ 개	
⓮ remove		㉞ 눈	
⓯ frown		㉟ 코	
⓰ face		㊱ 귀	
⓱ mouth		㊲ 달리다, 뛰다	
⓲ nervous		㊳ 걷다	
⓳ protect		㊴ 부르다, 전화하다	
⓴ bare		㊵ 오리	

Part 2

FINISH

START

Day 06 Arts

Check Up Read and check the words you don't know.

1차 복습

☐ face   ☐ ear

☐ eye   ☐ nervous

☐ nose   ☐ protect

☐ mouth   ☐ bare

2차 복습

☐ bird   ☐ horse

☐ enemy   ☐ follow

※ **망각 제로!** 1일 전 3일 전 학습한 단어를 복습해요.

face 얼굴	**eye** 눈	**nose** 코	**mouth** 입
ear 귀	**nervous** 불안해하는	**protect** 보호하다, 지키다	**bare** 맨, 벌거벗은
bird 새	**enemy** 적	**horse** 말	**follow** 따라가다

We are superheroes!

Dennis's favorite color is red.

데니스가 가장 좋아하는 색은 _____이에요.

Rod is wearing a blue cape.

로드는 _____ 망토를 입고 있어요.

☐ 노란색(의)

☐ 빨간색(의)

☐ 파란색(의)

☐ 초록색(의)

Listen, say, and color.

Read &Write

Write the **Basic Words** and **Jump Up Words**.

	Apples are red. ⓐ ⓝ
red 빨간색(의)	사과는 빨간색이에요. _____ - - - - - - - - - - - - - - - - _____

	Bananas are yellow. ⓐ ⓝ
yellow 노란색(의)	바나나는 노란색이에요. _____ - - - - - - - - - - - - - - - - _____

	He has green eyes. ⓐ ⓝ
green 초록색(의)	그는 초록색 눈을 가지고 있어요. _____ - - - - - - - - - - - - - - - - _____

blue
파란색(의)

The sky is blue. @ⓝ

하늘은 파란색이에요.

---

color
색깔

What is your favorite color? ⓝ

가장 좋아하는 색깔이 무엇인가요?

---

create
창작하다,
창조하다

She created the music. ⓥ

그녀가 그 음악을 창작했어요.

---

symbol
상징

They are symbols of peace. ⓝ

그것들은 평화의 상징이에요.

---

carve
조각하다

He carves stone. ⓥ

그는 돌을 조각해요.

A Circle and trace the words.

1

노란색(의)	빨간색(의)

red

2

노란색(의)	초록색(의)

yellow

3

초록색(의)	파란색(의)

blue

B Unscramble and write the words.

1 색깔

c o r l o

2 상징

y s m o l b

3 초록색(의)

e r e g n

4 창작하다,
창조하다

e a r c t e

C Connect and fill in the blanks.

1

They are symbols of peace.

그것들은 평화의 _____이에요.

2

He carves stone.

그는 돌을 _____.

3

What is your favorite color?

가장 좋아하는 _____이 무엇인가요?

D Circle the words and complete the sentences.

1 바나나는 노란색이에요.

| green | yellow |

Bananas are _____.

2 그는 초록색 눈을 가지고 있어요.

| green | blue |

He has _____ eyes.

Day 07 House

Check UP Read and check the words you don't know.

1차 복습

- [ ] red
- [ ] yellow
- [ ] green
- [ ] blue

- [ ] color
- [ ] create
- [ ] symbol
- [ ] carve

2차 복습

- [ ] walk
- [ ] run

- [ ] argue
- [ ] remove

3차 복습

- [ ] happy
- [ ] sad

- [ ] sick
- [ ] grateful

※ 망각 제로! 1일 전 3일 전 7일 전 학습한 단어를 복습해요.

Word Tip

red 빨간색(의)	**yellow** 노란색(의)	**green** 초록색(의)	**blue** 파란색(의)
color 색깔	**create** 창작하다, 창조하다	**symbol** 상징	**carve** 조각하다
walk 걷다	**run** 달리다, 뛰다	**argue** 다투다, 언쟁하다	**remove** 벗다, 치우다
happy 행복한	**sad** 슬픈	**sick** 아픈	**grateful** 감사하는, 고마워하는

Rod has friends over.

Pop Quiz **Choose and check the right words.**

Kiara thinks Rod's desk is big.

키아라는 로드의 _____ 이 크다고 생각해요.

☐ 책상
☐ 열쇠

Dennis and Mong are jumping on Rod's bed.

데니스와 몽은 로드의 _____ 에서 뛰고 있어요.

☐ 침대
☐ 방

Catch Up

 **Listen & Say** Listen, say, and color.

 Read & Write Write the **Basic Words** and **Jump Up Words**.

| bed
침대 | **He lay in bed.** n
그는 침대에 누웠어요.
_____
- - - - - - - - - - -
_____  |

| chair
의자 | **I sat on a chair.** n
나는 의자에 앉았어요.
_____
- - - - - - - - - - -
_____ |

| desk
책상 | **My desk is tidy.** n
내 책상은 깨끗해요.
_____
- - - - - - - - - - -
_____  |

key
열쇠

I lost my key.

나는 열쇠를 잃어버렸어요.

_____

- -

_____

room
방

This is my room.

이것은 제 방이에요.

_____

- -

_____

instrument
악기, 기구

He can play musical instruments.

그는 악기들을 연주할 수 있어요.

_____

- -

_____

temperature
온도

The temperature **drops at night.**

밤에는 기온이 내려가요.

_____

- -

_____

blanket
담요

He washed his blanket.

그는 담요를 빨았어요.

_____

- -

_____

A Circle and write the words.

1

2

3

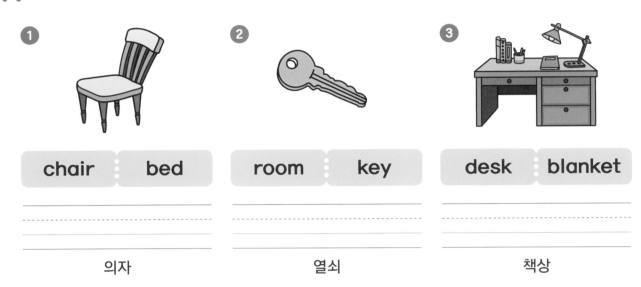

chair : bed	room : key	desk : blanket
_____	_____	_____
의자	열쇠	책상

B Connect and write the words.

1 blanket • • 침대 _____

2 room • • 방 _____

3 bed • • 악기, 기구 _____

4 instrument • • 담요 _____

54

C Connect, choose, and complete the sentences.

bed	room	temperature

1

이것은 제 방이에요.

This is my _____.

2

밤에는 기온이 내려가요.

The _____ drops at night.

3

그는 침대에 누웠어요.

He lay in _____.

D Circle the words and complete the sentences.

1 나는 의자에 앉았어요.

chair   desk

I sat on a _____.

2 그는 담요를 빨았어요.

instrument   blanket

He washed his _____.

Day 08 Animals

Read and check the words you don't know.

1차 복습

- [ ] bed
- [ ] chair
- [ ] desk
- [ ] key
- [ ] room
- [ ] instrument
- [ ] temperature
- [ ] blanket

2차 복습

- [ ] eye
- [ ] mouth
- [ ] bare
- [ ] protect

3차 복습

- [ ] family
- [ ] brother
- [ ] host
- [ ] polite

※망각 제로! 1일 전 3일 전 7일 전 학습한 단어를 복습해요.

Word Tip

bed 침대	chair 의자	desk 책상	key 열쇠
room 방	instrument 악기, 기구	temperature 온도	blanket 담요
eye 눈	mouth 입	bare 맨, 벌거벗은	protect 보호하다, 지키다
family 가족	brother 남자 형제	host 주인, 주최하다	polite 공손한

56

Are tigers stronger than lions?

Choose and check the right words.

Sally thinks lions are fierce.

샐리는 사자가 ＿＿＿＿＿＿고 생각해요.

☐ 동물원

☐ 사나운

Rod said tigers have sharp claws.

로드는 호랑이가 ＿＿＿＿＿＿ 발톱을 가지고 있다고 말했어요.

☐ 날카로운

☐ 기린

Read & Write

Write the **Basic Words** and **Jump Up Words**.

zoo 동물원	**They are at the zoo.** 그들은 동물원에 있어요.
lion 사자	**I see a lion.** 나는 사자를 봐요.
tiger 호랑이	**The tiger is scary.** 그 호랑이는 무서워요.

rabbit
토끼

The rabbit has brown fur. n

그 토끼는 갈색 털을 가지고 있어요.

_____
- - - - - - - - - - - - - - - -
_____

giraffe
기린

The giraffe is eating leaves. n

기린이 잎을 먹고 있어요.

_____
- - - - - - - - - - - - - - - -
_____

fierce
사나운, 격렬한

The dog looks fierce. a

그 개는 사나워 보여요.

_____
- - - - - - - - - - - - - - - -
_____

sharp
날카로운

A tiger has sharp teeth. a

호랑이는 날카로운 이빨을 가지고 있어요.

_____
- - - - - - - - - - - - - - - -
_____

attack
공격하다

A lion attacked a man. v

사자가 남자를 공격했어요.

_____
- - - - - - - - - - - - - - - -
_____

Skill UP

A Circle the letters and complete the words.

1

h g j z

_ _ o o

동물원

2

i t a g

_ i _ e r

호랑이

3

s t h g

_ _ a r p

날카로운

B Find, circle, and write the words.

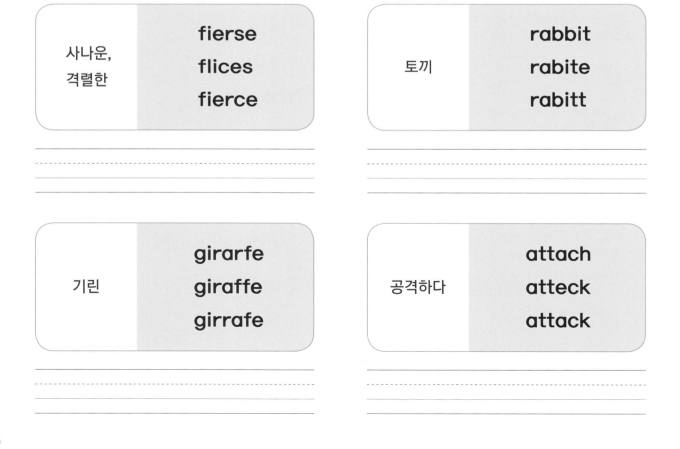

사나운, 격렬한	fierse flices fierce

토끼	rabbit rabite rabitt

기린	girarfe giraffe girrafe

공격하다	attach atteck attack

C Connect and fill in the blanks.

①

The **rabbit** has brown fur.

그 _____는 갈색 털을 가지고 있어요.

②

I see a **lion**.

나는 _____를 봐요.

③

The **giraffe** is eating leaves.

_____이 잎을 먹고 있어요.

D Choose and complete the sentences.

fierce	zoo	sharp

① 그들은 동물원에 있어요.

They are at the _____.

② 그 개는 사나워 보여요.

The dog looks _____.

③ 호랑이는 날카로운 이빨을 가지고 있어요.

A tiger has _____ teeth.

Day 09 Descriptive Words

Check Up Read and check the words you don't know.

1차 복습

- [ ] zoo
- [ ] lion
- [ ] tiger
- [ ] rabbit
- [ ] giraffe
- [ ] fierce
- [ ] sharp
- [ ] attack

2차 복습

- [ ] color
- [ ] red
- [ ] create
- [ ] carve

3차 복습

- [ ] cat
- [ ] dog
- [ ] duck
- [ ] various

※ 망각 제로! 1일 전 3일 전 7일 전 학습한 단어를 복습해요.

Word Tip

zoo 동물원
lion 사자
tiger 호랑이
rabbit 토끼
giraffe 기린
fierce 사나운, 격렬한
sharp 날카로운
attack 공격하다
color 색깔
red 빨간색(의)
create 창작하다, 창조하다
carve 조각하다
cat 고양이
dog 개
duck 오리
various 다양한, 여러 가지의

Let's pick apples.

Pop Quiz Choose and check the right words.

Rod picked a small apple.

로드는 ＿＿＿＿＿＿＿＿ 사과를 땄어요.

☐ 큰

☐ 작은

Kiara has long arms.

키아라는 팔이 ＿＿＿＿＿＿＿＿요.

☐ 짧은

☐ 긴

Catch Up

 **Listen, say, and color.**

Read & Write Write the **Basic Words** and **Jump Up Words**.

| big 큰 | **An elephant is big.**
 코끼리는 커요.
 _____
 - - - - - - - - - - -
 _____ | a |

| small 작은 | **A mouse is small.**
 쥐는 작아요.
 _____
 - - - - - - - - - - -
 _____ | a |

| fast 빠르게, 빠른 | **A cheetah runs fast.**
 치타는 빠르게 달려요.
 _____
 - - - - - - - - - - -
 _____ | ad a |

long
긴

She has long hair. a

그녀는 머리카락이 길어요.

short
짧은

The yellow jump rope is short. a

노란 줄넘기는 짧아요.

edge
끝, 모서리

He stood on the edge of the cliff. n

그는 벼랑 끝에 서 있었어요.

enormous
거대한

Their house is enormous. a

그들의 집은 거대해요.

smooth
매끄러운

He has smooth skin. a

그는 매끄러운 피부를 가지고 있어요.

A Circle and trace the words.

1

큰 : 작은

big

2

빠르게 : 거대한

fast

3

긴 : 짧은

short

B Connect and write the words.

1 edge • • 거대한 ____

2 smooth • • 긴 ____

3 enormous • • 매끄러운 ____

4 long • • 끝, 모서리 ____

66

C Connect, choose, and complete the sentences.

small	edge	enormous

1

그는 벼랑 끝에 서 있었어요.

He stood on the _____ of the cliff.

2

그들의 집은 거대해요.

Their house is _____.

3

쥐는 작아요.

A mouse is _____.

D Circle the words and complete the sentences.

1 그녀는 머리카락이 길어요.

short	long

She has _____ hair.

2 그는 매끄러운 피부를 가지고 있어요.

enormous	smooth

He has _____ skin.

Day 10 Food

Check UP Read and check the words you don't know.

1차 복습

- ☐ big
- ☐ small
- ☐ fast
- ☐ long

- ☐ short
- ☐ edge
- ☐ enormous
- ☐ smooth

2차 복습

- ☐ bed
- ☐ desk

- ☐ room
- ☐ temperature

3차 복습

- ☐ sing
- ☐ dance

- ☐ argue
- ☐ frown

※ **망각 제로!** 1일 전 3일 전 7일 전 학습한 단어를 복습해요.

big 큰	**small** 작은	**fast** 빠르게, 빠른	**long** 긴
short 짧은	**edge** 끝, 모서리	**enormous** 거대한	**smooth** 매끄러운
bed 침대	**desk** 책상	**room** 방	**temperature** 온도
sing 노래하다	**dance** 춤추다	**argue** 다투다, 언쟁하다	**frown** 눈살을 찌푸리다

Rod makes sandwiches.

POP Quiz Choose and check the right words.

Rod spread butter on some bread.

로드는 _____에 버터를 발랐어요.

□ 빵

□ 고기

Rod added eggs to the sandwiches.

로드는 샌드위치에 _____을 추가했어요.

□ 달걀

□ 생선

 **Listen, say, and color.**

Read & Write **Write the Basic Words and Jump Up Words.**

fish
생선

I like fish.

나는 생선을 좋아해요.

_____

_____

_____

meat
고기

He is eating meat.

그는 고기를 먹고 있어요.

_____

_____

_____

bread
빵

She ate bread with jam.

그녀는 잼을 바른 빵을 먹었어요.

_____

_____

_____

egg
달걀

I like boiled eggs.

나는 삶은 달걀을 좋아해요.

milk
우유

I drink milk.

나는 우유를 마셔요.

wrap
포장하다, 싸다

He wrapped **the sandwich.**

그는 샌드위치를 포장했어요.

spread
바르다, 펴다

I spread **butter on the bread.**

나는 빵에 버터를 발랐어요.

chew
씹다

She is chewing **gum.**

그녀는 껌을 씹고 있어요.

A Circle and write the words.

1

fish | egg

_____

달걀

2

milk | bread

_____

우유

3

fish | bread

_____

생선

B Unscramble and write the words.

1 씹다   h w c e   _____

2 포장하다, 싸다   a r w p   _____

3 고기   t e a m   _____

4 바르다, 펴다   p r e d s a   _____

C Connect and fill in the blanks.

1

He is eating meat.

그는 _____를 먹고 있어요.

2

She is chewing **gum.**

그녀는 껌을 _____ 있어요.

3

She ate bread **with jam.**

그녀는 잼을 바른 _____을 먹었어요.

D Choose and complete the sentences.

wrapped	eggs	fish

1 나는 생선을 좋아해요.

I like _____.

2 그는 샌드위치를 포장했어요.

He _____ the sandwich.

3 나는 삶은 달걀을 좋아해요.

I like boiled _____.

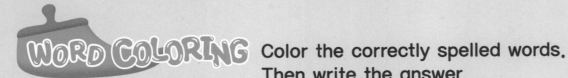
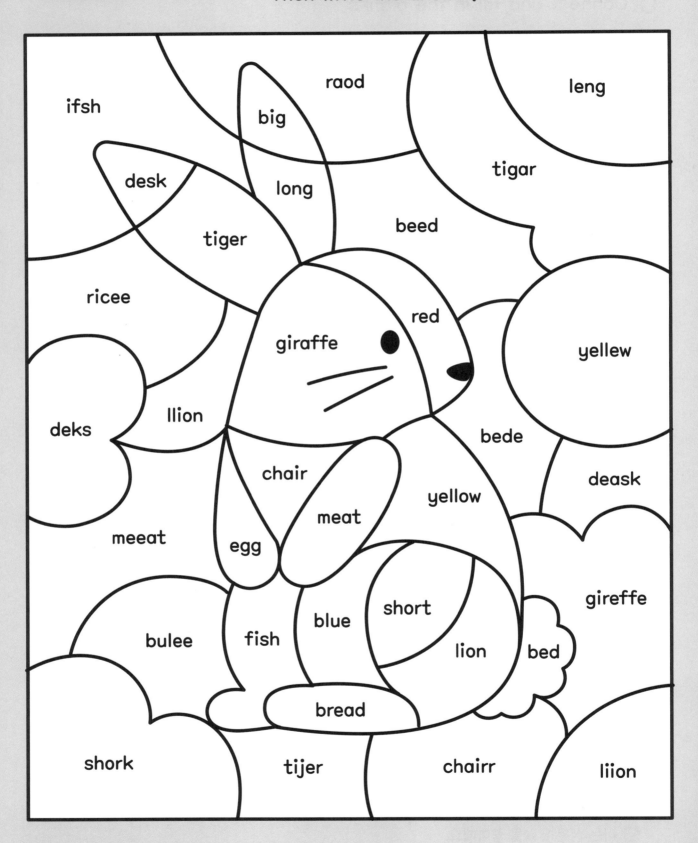

Q. What animal do you see?

red 빨간색(의)	**yellow** 노란색(의)	**green** 초록색(의)	**blue** 파란색(의)	**color** 색깔
create 창작하다, 창조하다	**symbol** 상징	**carve** 조각하다	**bed** 침대	**chair** 의자
desk 책상	**key** 열쇠	**room** 방	**instrument** 악기, 기구	**temperature** 온도
blanket 담요	**zoo** 동물원	**lion** 사자	**tiger** 호랑이	**rabbit** 토끼
giraffe 기린	**fierce** 사나운, 격렬한	**sharp** 날카로운	**attack** 공격하다	**big** 큰
small 작은	**fast** 빠르게, 빠른	**long** 긴	**short** 짧은	**edge** 끝, 모서리
enormous 거대한	**smooth** 매끄러운	**fish** 생선	**meat** 고기	**bread** 빵
egg 달걀	**milk** 우유	**wrap** 포장하다, 싸다	**spread** 바르다, 펴다	**chew** 씹다

Day 06~10

맞힌 개수 : ☐ /40

❶ red		㉑ 초록색(의)	
❷ yellow		㉒ 파란색(의)	
❸ symbol		㉓ 색깔	
❹ create		㉔ 조각하다	
❺ bed		㉕ 책상	
❻ chair		㉖ 열쇠	
❼ temperature		㉗ 방	
❽ blanket		㉘ 악기, 기구	
❾ zoo		㉙ 호랑이	
❿ lion		㉚ 토끼	
⓫ fierce		㉛ 기린	
⓬ attack		㉜ 날카로운	
⓭ big		㉝ 빠르게, 빠른	
⓮ small		㉞ 긴	
⓯ enormous		㉟ 짧은	
⓰ smooth		㊱ 끝, 모서리	
⓱ fish		㊲ 빵	
⓲ meat		㊳ 달걀	
⓳ spread		㊴ 우유	
⓴ chew		㊵ 포장하다, 싸다	

Part 3

FINISH

START

Day 11 Society

Check Up Read and check the words you don't know.

1차 복습

☐ fish   ☐ milk
☐ meat   ☐ wrap
☐ bread   ☐ spread
☐ egg   ☐ chew

2차 복습

☐ zoo   ☐ giraffe
☐ lion   ☐ fierce

3차 복습

☐ face   ☐ protect
☐ mouth   ☐ bare

※ 망각 제로! 1일 전 3일 전 7일 전 학습한 단어를 복습해요.

Word Tip

fish 생선	**meat** 고기	**bread** 빵	**egg** 달걀
milk 우유	**wrap** 포장하다, 싸다	**spread** 바르다, 펴다	**chew** 씹다
zoo 동물원	**lion** 사자	**giraffe** 기린	**fierce** 사나운, 격렬한
face 얼굴	**mouth** 입	**protect** 보호하다, 지키다	**bare** 맨, 벌거벗은

We are at the amusement park.

Pop Quiz Choose and check the right words.

**There are many people
at the amusement park.**

놀이공원에 _____이 아주 많아요.

☐ 사람들

☐ 아기

Kiara knows the person with sunglasses.

키아라는 선글라스를 낀 _____을 알고 있어요.

☐ 또래

☐ 사람

 Listen, say, and color.

 Write the **Basic Words** and **Jump Up Words**.

| boy
남자아이 | **Look at the boy.**
남자아이를 보세요.

_____
_____
_____ |

Look at the boy.
남자아이를 보세요.

The girl is smiling.
여자아이가 웃고 있어요.

girl
여자아이

I know the man.
나는 그 남자를 알아요.

man
남자

80

woman
여자

The woman is famous.
그 여자는 유명해요.

---

baby
아기

The baby is crawling.
아기가 기어가고 있어요.

---

peer
또래

I get along well with my peers.
나는 또래들과 잘 어울려요.

---

person
사람

There was one person in the room.
그 방에는 한 사람이 있었어요.

---

people
사람들

There were a lot of people at the party.
그 파티에는 많은 사람들이 있었어요.

Skill UP

A Circle and trace the words.

1

| 여자아이 | 남자아이 |

boy

2

| 여자 | 남자 |

man

3

| 아기 | 또래 |

baby

B Find, circle, and write the words.

여자	weman
	woman
	wuman

_____

사람	person
	pelson
	parson

_____

사람들	peeple
	people
	paople

_____

또래	peer
	feer
	pear

_____

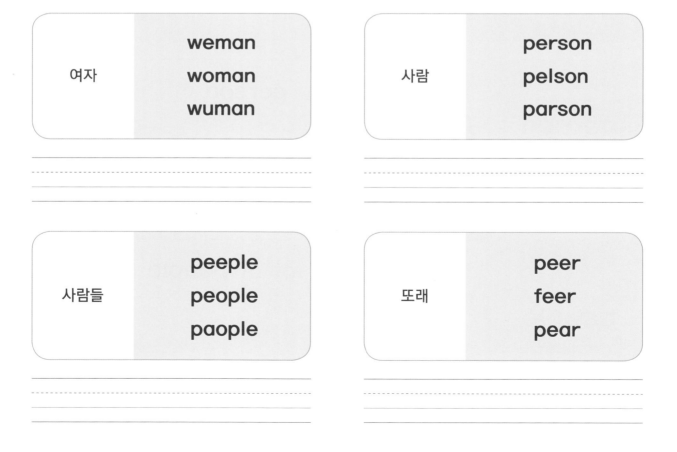

C Connect, choose, and complete the sentences.

peers	people	girl

1

여자아이가 웃고 있어요.

The _____ is smiling.

2

나는 또래들과 잘 어울려요.

I get along well
with my _____.

3

그 파티에는 많은 사람들이 있었어요.

There were a lot of
_____ at the party.

D Circle the words and complete the sentences.

1 그 여자는 유명해요.   man ⋮ woman

The _____ is famous.

2 그 방에는 한 사람이 있었어요.   people ⋮ person

There was one _____ in the room.

Day 12 Nature

Check Up Read and check the words you don't know.

1차 복습

- [ ] boy
- [ ] girl
- [ ] man
- [ ] woman
- [ ] baby
- [ ] peer
- [ ] person
- [ ] people

2차 복습

- [ ] long
- [ ] short
- [ ] enormous
- [ ] smooth

3차 복습

- [ ] blue
- [ ] color
- [ ] symbol
- [ ] carve

※ **망각 제로!** 1일 전 3일 전 7일 전 학습한 단어를 복습해요.

Word Tip

boy 남자아이	**girl** 여자아이	**man** 남자	**woman** 여자
baby 아기	**peer** 또래	**person** 사람	**people** 사람들
long 긴	**short** 짧은	**enormous** 거대한	**smooth** 매끄러운
blue 파란색(의)	**color** 색깔	**symbol** 상징	**carve** 조각하다

What a beautiful sunrise!

Pop Quiz Choose and check the right words.

Kiara said the sky was still dark.

키아라는 _____이 아직 깜깜하다고 했어요.

☐ 달

☐ 하늘

Rod told his friends not to stare at the sun.

로드는 친구들에게 해를 _____ 말라고 말했어요.

☐ 빠히 쳐다보다

☐ 날이 밝다

Read & Write Write the **Basic Words** and **Jump Up Words**.

sky 하늘	**The sky is clear today.** 오늘은 하늘이 맑아요. 

sun 해, 태양	**The sun is shining.** 해가 빛나고 있어요.

moon 달	**The moon is bright.** 달이 밝아요. 

star
별

Look at the brightest star. **n**

가장 빛나는 별을 보세요.

_____

_____

_____

wind
바람

The wind **is cold.** **n**

바람이 차요.

_____

_____

_____

stare
응시하다,
빤히 쳐다보다

She is staring **at the sea.** **v**

그녀는 바다를 응시하고 있어요.

_____

_____

_____

dawn
새벽,
날이 밝다

It is almost dawn. **n** **v**

새벽이 거의 다 되었어요.

_____

_____

_____

soil
흙

Cover the seeds with soil. **n**

흙으로 씨를 덮으세요.

_____

_____

_____

Skill UP

A Circle the letters and complete the words.

1

a o u e

s _ n

해, 태양

2

o u o a

m _ _ n

달

3

c t s k

_ a r

별

B Unscramble and write the words.

1 새벽,
날이 밝다

a d n w

_____

2 흙

s o l i

_____

3 하늘

s y k

_____

4 응시하다,
빤히 쳐다보다

e t a r s

_____

88

C Connect and fill in the blanks.

1

The wind is cold.

_____이 차요.

2

It is almost dawn.

_____이 거의 다 되었어요.

3

Cover the seeds with soil.

_____으로 씨를 덮으세요.

D Choose and complete the sentences.

sky	star	moon

1 오늘은 하늘이 맑아요.

The _____ is clear today.

2 달이 밝아요.

The _____ is bright.

3 가장 빛나는 별을 보세요.

Look at the brightest _____.

Day 13 Individuality

Check Up Read and check the words you don't know.

1차 복습

- [ ] sky
- [ ] sun
- [ ] moon
- [ ] star
- [ ] wind
- [ ] stare
- [ ] dawn
- [ ] soil

2차 복습

- [ ] egg
- [ ] milk
- [ ] wrap
- [ ] spread

3차 복습

- [ ] room
- [ ] instrument
- [ ] temperature
- [ ] blanket

※ **망각 제로!** 1일 전 3일 전 7일 전 학습한 단어를 복습해요.

Word Tip

sky 하늘	**sun** 해, 태양	**moon** 달	**star** 별
wind 바람	**stare** 응시하다, 빤히 쳐다보다	**dawn** 새벽, 날이 밝다	**soil** 흙
egg 달걀	**milk** 우유	**wrap** 포장하다, 싸다	**spread** 바르다, 펴다
room 방	**instrument** 악기, 기구	**temperature** 온도	**blanket** 담요

Kiara fell in love!

Pop Quiz Choose and check the right words.

The boy said the flowers were pretty.

남자아이는 꽃이 _____고 했어요.

Sally thinks the boy is cute and tall.

샐리는 남자아이가 귀엽고 _____고 생각해요.

- [ ] 예쁜
- [ ] 어린
- [ ] 키가 큰
- [ ] 키가 작은

Listen & Say — Listen, say, and color.

Read & Write — Write the **Basic Words** and **Jump Up Words**.

tall 키가 큰	**She is tall.** 그녀는 키가 커요. _____ _____ _____

cute 귀여운	**He is cute.** 그는 귀여워요. _____ _____ _____

old 나이가 든, 낡은	**She is old.** 그녀는 나이가 많아요. _____ _____ _____

young
어린, 젊은

He is young. a

그는 어려요.

_____
- - - - - - - - - - - - - - - - -
_____

pretty
예쁜

She is pretty. a

그녀는 예뻐요.

_____
- - - - - - - - - - - - - - - - -
_____

beauty
아름다움

I love the beauty **of her face.** n

나는 아름다운 그녀의 얼굴을 좋아해요.

_____
- - - - - - - - - - - - - - - - -
_____

tense
긴장한,
신경이 날카로운

He looks tense. a

그는 긴장한 것 같아요.

_____
- - - - - - - - - - - - - - - - -
_____

rude
무례한, 버릇없는

Don't be rude. a

무례하게 굴지 마세요.

_____
- - - - - - - - - - - - - - - - -
_____

A Circle and write the words.

1

cute : rude

_____

귀여운

2

young : old

_____

나이가 든, 낡은

3

pretty : tense

_____

예쁜

B Connect and write the words.

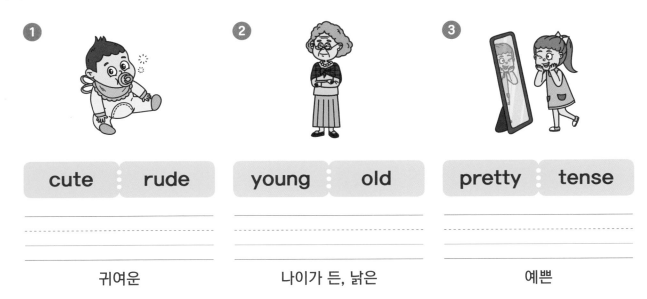

1 young •

2 rude •

3 tense •

4 beauty •

• 무례한, 버릇없는 _____

• 어린, 젊은 _____

• 아름다움 _____

• 긴장한, 신경이 날카로운 _____

C Connect, choose, and complete the sentences.

young	tall	tense

1

그는 어려요.

He is _____.

2

그녀는 키가 커요.

She is _____.

3

그는 긴장한 것 같아요.

He looks _____.

D Circle the words and complete the sentences.

1 무례하게 굴지 마세요.

tense	rude

Don't be _____.

2 그녀는 예뻐요.

pretty	beauty

She is _____.

Day 14 Time

Check Up Read and check the words you don't know.

1차 복습

- ☐ tall
- ☐ cute
- ☐ old
- ☐ young
- ☐ pretty
- ☐ beauty
- ☐ tense
- ☐ rude

2차 복습

- ☐ baby
- ☐ peer
- ☐ person
- ☐ people

3차 복습

- ☐ tiger
- ☐ sharp
- ☐ rabbit
- ☐ attack

※망각 제로! 1일 전 3일 전 7일 전 학습한 단어를 복습해요.

Word Tip

tall 키가 큰　　　**cute** 귀여운　　　**old** 나이가 든, 낡은　　　**young** 어린, 젊은

pretty 예쁜　　　**beauty** 아름다움　　　**tense** 긴장한, 신경이 날카로운　　　**rude** 무례한, 버릇없는

baby 아기　　　**peer** 또래　　　**person** 사람　　　**people** 사람들

tiger 호랑이　　　**sharp** 날카로운　　　**rabbit** 토끼　　　**attack** 공격하다

Mong had a wonderful day.

![PopQuiz] **Choose and check the right words.**

Mong visited Kiara's house in the morning.

몽은 _____에 키아라의 집에 갔어요.

- ☐ 아침
- ☐ 저녁

Mong met Dennis in the afternoon.

몽은 _____에 데니스를 만났어요.

- ☐ 밤
- ☐ 오후

 Listen, say, and color.

Read & Write Write the **Basic Words** and **Jump Up Words**.

morning 아침	**Good** morning. 좋은 아침이에요. _____ _____	

afternoon 오후	**Good** afternoon. 좋은 오후예요. _____ _____	

evening 저녁	**Good** evening. 좋은 저녁이에요. _____ _____	

night
밤

Good night.

(밤의 취침·작별 인사) 잘 자요.

_____

n

noon
정오
(낮 열두 시)

I have lunch at noon.

나는 정오에 점심을 먹어요.

_____

n

beam
광선, 빛줄기

Look at the beam **of sunlight.**

햇빛의 광선을 보세요.

_____

n

gather
모이다

They gathered **to take pictures.**

그들은 사진을 찍기 위해 모였어요.

_____

v

silent
조용한

Please be silent.

조용히 해주세요.

_____

a

Skill UP

A Circle and trace the words.

①	②	③
아침 : 오후	밤 : 저녁	밤 : 정오
morning	evening	night

B Unscramble and write the words.

① 정오
(낮 열두 시)

n o n o

_____

② 광선, 빛줄기

m a e b

_____

③ 모이다

g t a e r h

_____

④ 조용한

l e n i s t

_____

100

C Connect and fill in the blanks.

1

Good afternoon.

좋은 _____예요.

2

I have lunch at noon.

나는 _____에 점심을 먹어요.

3

Look at the beam of sunlight.

햇빛의 _____을 보세요.

D Choose and complete the sentences.

silent   gathered   morning

1 좋은 아침이에요.

Good _____.

2 조용히 해주세요.

Please be _____.

3 그들은 사진을 찍기 위해 모였어요.

They _____ to take pictures.

Check Up Read and check the words you don't know.

1차 복습

☐ morning
☐ afternoon
☐ evening
☐ night

☐ noon
☐ beam
☐ gather
☐ silent

2차 복습

☐ moon
☐ star

☐ stare
☐ dawn

3차 복습

☐ edge
☐ smooth

☐ fast
☐ long

※ 망각 제로! 1일 전 3일 전 7일 전 학습한 단어를 복습해요.

 Word Tip

morning 아침	afternoon 오후	evening 저녁	night 밤
noon 정오(낮 열두 시)	beam 광선, 빛줄기	gather 모이다	silent 조용한
moon 달	star 별	stare 응시하다, 빤히 쳐다보다	dawn 새벽, 날이 밝다
edge 끝, 모서리	smooth 매끄러운	fast 빠르게, 빠른	long 긴

What do you want to be?

 Choose and check the right words.

The students are imagining what they want to be.

학생들은 무엇이 되고 싶은지 _____ 있어요.

- [ ] 상상하다
- [ ] 심판하다

Kiara wants to be a doctor.

키아라는 _____가 되고 싶어 해요.

- [ ] 간호사
- [ ] 의사

Listen, say, and color.

Read & Write

Write the **Basic Words** and **Jump Up Words**.

doctor 의사	**I am a doctor.** n 나는 의사예요. _____ _____ _____ 

nurse 간호사	**A nurse looks after people.** n 간호사는 사람들을 돌봐요. _____ _____ _____

cook 요리사, 요리하다	**He works as a cook.** n v 그는 요리사로 일해요. _____ _____ _____ 

clerk
점원, 직원

He is a clerk at a shoe store. [n]
그는 신발 가게 점원이에요.

---

business
사업, 업무

She runs a business. [n]
그녀는 사업을 해요.

---

judge
판사, 심판

She is a high court judge. [n]
그녀는 고등법원 판사예요.

---

fair
공평한, 공정한

Life isn't always fair. [a]
인생이 항상 공평한 것은 아니에요.

---

imagine
상상하다

I imagine being a millionaire. [v]
나는 백만장자가 되는 것을 상상해요.

A Circle and write the words.

①	②	③
nurse : doctor	judge : cook	cook : clerk

의사   요리사, 요리하다   점원, 직원

B Find, circle, and write the words.

판사, 심판	jadge gudge judge

사업, 업무	business bussines bisiness

상상하다	imegine imajine imagine

공평한, 공정한	feir fair feer

C Connect, choose, and complete the sentences.

| judge | business | imagine |

1

나는 백만장자가 되는 것을 상상해요.

I _____ being a millionaire.

2

그녀는 고등법원 판사예요.

She is a high court _____.

3

그녀는 사업을 해요.

She runs a _____.

D Circle the words and complete the sentences.

1 간호사는 사람들을 돌봐요.

nurse   judge

A _____ looks after people.

2 그는 요리사로 일해요.

clerk   cook

He works as a _____ .

WORD PUZZLE Complete the word puzzle. Then write the sentence.

Word Bank

boy · business · doctor · girl
moon · night · old · sun · young

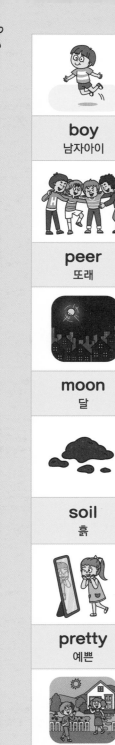				
boy 남자아이	**girl** 여자아이	**man** 남자	**woman** 여자	**baby** 아기
peer 또래	**person** 사람	**people** 사람들	**sky** 하늘	**sun** 해, 태양
moon 달	**star** 별	**wind** 바람	**stare** 응시하다, 빤히 쳐다보다	**dawn** 새벽, 날이 밝다
soil 흙	**tall** 키가 큰	**cute** 귀여운	**old** 나이가 든, 낡은	**young** 어린, 젊은
pretty 예쁜	**beauty** 아름다움	**tense** 긴장한, 신경이 날카로운	**rude** 무례한, 버릇없는	**morning** 아침
afternoon 오후	**evening** 저녁	**night** 밤	**noon** 정오(낮 열두 시)	**beam** 광선, 빛줄기
gather 모이다	**silent** 조용한	**doctor** 의사	**nurse** 간호사	**cook** 요리사, 요리하다
clerk 점원, 직원	**business** 사업, 업무	**judge** 판사, 심판	**fair** 공평한, 공정한	**imagine** 상상하다

Review TEST

맞힌 개수 : ☐ / 40

❶ boy		㉑ 남자	
❷ girl		㉒ 여자	
❸ person		㉓ 또래	
❹ people		㉔ 아기	
❺ sky		㉕ 달	
❻ sun		㉖ 별	
❼ dawn		㉗ 바람	
❽ stare		㉘ 흙	
❾ old		㉙ 키가 큰	
❿ cute		㉚ 어린, 젊은	
⓫ tense		㉛ 예쁜	
⓬ rude		㉜ 아름다움	
⓭ morning		㉝ 저녁	
⓮ afternoon		㉞ 밤	
⓯ gather		㉟ 정오(낮 열두 시)	
⓰ silent		㊱ 광선, 빛줄기	
⓱ cook		㊲ 의사	
⓲ nurse		㊳ 점원, 직원	
⓳ fair		㊴ 판사, 심판	
⓴ business		㊵ 상상하다	

Part 4

FINISH

START

Check Up Read and check the words you don't know.

1차 복습

☐ doctor	☐ business
☐ nurse	☐ judge
☐ cook	☐ fair
☐ clerk	☐ imagine

2차 복습

☐ young	☐ cute
☐ pretty	☐ rude

3차 복습

☐ fish	☐ wrap
☐ meat	☐ spread

※ 망각 제로! 1일 전 3일 전 7일 전 학습한 단어를 복습해요.

doctor 의사

business 사업, 업무

young 어린, 젊은

fish 생선

nurse 간호사

judge 판사, 심판

pretty 예쁜

meat 고기

cook 요리사, 요리하다

fair 공평한, 공정한

cute 귀여운

wrap 포장하다, 싸다

clerk 점원, 직원

imagine 상상하다

rude 무례한, 버릇없는

spread 바르다, 펴다

What's your favorite flavor?

Pop Quiz Choose and check the right words.

Rod wants rice ice cream with honey.

로드는 ＿＿＿＿＿＿이 추가된 쌀 아이스크림을 원해요.

☐ 꿀

☐ 음식

Kiara spotted an empty table.

키아라가 ＿＿＿＿＿＿ 테이블을 발견했어요.

☐ 비어 있는

☐ 불평하는

 Write the **Basic Words** and **Jump Up Words**.

rice 밥, 쌀	ⓝ **I have rice for lunch every day.** 나는 점심으로 매일 밥을 먹어요. 
honey 꿀	ⓝ **I love honey on toast.** 나는 토스트에 꿀 바른 것을 좋아해요.
food 음식	ⓝ **The food is yummy.** 음식이 맛있어요. 

bottle
병

We need a bottle of ketchup. (n)

우리는 케첩 한 병이 필요해요.

_____

- - - - - - - - - - - - - - -

_____

cookie
쿠키

I made cookies. (n)

나는 쿠키를 만들었어요.

_____

- - - - - - - - - - - - - - -

_____

complain
불평하다

He is complaining about the food. (v)

그는 음식에 대해 불평하고 있어요.

_____

- - - - - - - - - - - - - - -

_____

empty
비어 있는, 빈

The fridge is empty. (a)

냉장고가 비어 있어요.

_____

- - - - - - - - - - - - - - -

_____

flavor
맛

I like chocolate flavor. (n)

나는 초콜릿 맛이 좋아요.

_____

- - - - - - - - - - - - - - -

_____

Skill UP

A Circle the letters and complete the words.

1

a e r i

r _ c _

밥, 쌀

2

h g m n

_ o _ e y

꿀

3

a o e o

f _ _ d

음식

B Unscramble and write the words.

1 병   t o t l b e   _____

2 맛   f v a l r o   _____

3 쿠키   e c o k o i   _____

4 불평하다   l m c o a i p n   _____

C Connect and fill in the blanks.

1

The fridge is empty.

냉장고가 _____요.

2

I like chocolate flavor.

나는 초콜릿 _____이 좋아요.

3

We need a bottle of ketchup.

우리는 케첩 한 _____이 필요해요.

D Choose and complete the sentences.

cookies	honey	rice

1 나는 점심으로 매일 밥을 먹어요.

I have _____ for lunch every day.

2 나는 쿠키를 만들었어요.

I made _____.

3 나는 토스트에 꿀 바른 것을 좋아해요.

I love _____ on toast.

Day 17 Body Actions

Check Up Read and check the words you don't know.

1차 복습

☐ rice	☐ cookie
☐ honey	☐ complain
☐ food	☐ empty
☐ bottle	☐ flavor

2차 복습

☐ morning	☐ noon
☐ evening	☐ night

3차 복습

☐ boy	☐ man
☐ girl	☐ woman

※ **망각 제로!** 1일 전 3일 전 7일 전 학습한 단어를 복습해요.

Word Tip

rice 밥, 쌀	**honey** 꿀	**food** 음식	**bottle** 병
cookie 쿠키	**complain** 불평하다	**empty** 비어 있는, 빈	**flavor** 맛
morning 아침	**evening** 저녁	**noon** 정오(낮 열두 시)	**night** 밤
boy 남자아이	**girl** 여자아이	**man** 남자	**woman** 여자

It's fun to take a plane.

Pop Quiz Choose and check the right words.

Dennis should open the window shade.

데니스는 창문 덮개를 _____ 해요.

- [ ] 닫다
- [ ] 열다

Passengers should fasten their seat belts.

승객들은 좌석 벨트를 _____ 해요.

- [ ] 매다
- [ ] 붙이다

Listen, say, and color.

Write the Basic Words and Jump Up Words.

| sit 앉다 | **Sit down, please.** ⓥ 앉으세요.  |

| stand 일어서다 | **Stand up, please.** ⓥ 일어서세요. |

| open 열다 | **He opens the window.** ⓥ 그는 창문을 열어요.  |

close
닫다

I close **the window.**

나는 창문을 닫아요.

_____

move
옮기다,
움직이다

We move **the boxes.**

우리는 상자들을 옮겨요.

_____

attach
붙이다

She attached **the photos.**

그녀는 사진들을 붙였어요.

_____

perform
공연하다,
수행하다

The children perform **a play.**

아이들이 연극을 공연해요.

_____

fasten
매다, 고정시키다

Fasten **your seat belt.**

안전벨트를 매세요.

_____

A Circle and trace the words.

1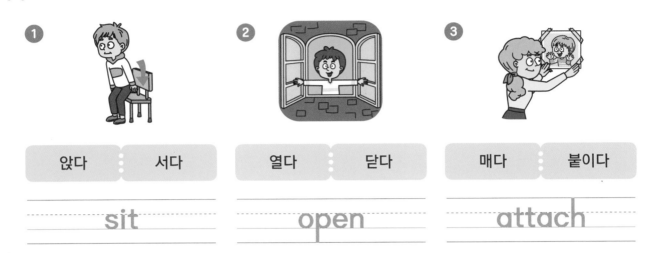

앉다	서다

sit

2

열다	닫다

open

3

매다	붙이다

attach

B Connect and write the words.

1 stand •

2 perform •

3 move •

4 fasten •

• 공연하다,
수행하다

• 옮기다,
움직이다

• 일어서다

• 매다,
고정시키다

C Connect, choose, and complete the sentences.

perform	close	Stand

1

나는 창문을 닫아요.

I _____ the window.

2

일어서세요.

_____ up, please.

3

아이들이 연극을 공연해요.

The children _____ a play.

D Circle the words and complete the sentences.

1 우리는 상자들을 옮겨요.

attach : move

We _____ the boxes.

2 안전벨트를 매세요.

Perform : Fasten

_____ your seat belt.

Check Up Read and check the words you don't know.

1차 복습

- [ ] sit
- [ ] stand
- [ ] open
- [ ] close
- [ ] move
- [ ] attach
- [ ] perform
- [ ] fasten

2차 복습

- [ ] doctor
- [ ] nurse
- [ ] cook
- [ ] clerk

3차 복습

- [ ] sky
- [ ] sun
- [ ] dawn
- [ ] soil

※ 망각 제로! 1일 전 3일 전 7일 전 학습한 단어를 복습해요.

Word Tip

sit 앉다	stand 일어서다	open 열다	close 닫다
move 옮기다, 움직이다	attach 붙이다	perform 공연하다, 수행하다	fasten 매다, 고정시키다
doctor 의사	nurse 간호사	cook 요리사, 요리하다	clerk 점원, 직원
sky 하늘	sun 해, 태양	dawn 새벽, 날이 밝다	soil 흙

Let's go catch insects!

Pop Quiz Choose and check the right words.

Kiara thinks the flowers are so beautiful.

키아라는 _____이 아주 아름답다고 생각해요.

☐ 산
☐ 꽃

Dennis and Mong climbed up a tree.

데니스와 몽은 _____ 위에 올라갔어요.

☐ 나무
☐ 해변

Listen & Say Listen, say, and color.

Read & Write Write the **Basic Words** and **Jump Up Words**.

flower 꽃	**We plant** flowers. 우리는 꽃을 심어요.

tree 나무	**We plant** trees. 우리는 나무를 심어요.

river 강	**I swam in the** river. 나는 강에서 수영했어요.

mountain 산	**(n)** **I climbed a mountain.** 나는 산을 올랐어요. _____ _____ _____

beach 해변	**(n)** **Look at the beach.** 해변을 보세요. _____ _____ _____

insect 곤충	**(n)** **I hate flying insects.** 나는 날아다니는 곤충을 싫어해요. _____ _____ _____

surround 둘러싸다, 에워싸다	**(v)** **The house is surrounded by trees.** 그 집은 나무로 둘러싸여 있어요. _____ _____ _____

plant 심다, 식물	**(v) (n)** **We plant tomatoes.** 우리는 토마토를 심어요. _____ _____ _____

Skill Up

A Circle and write the words.

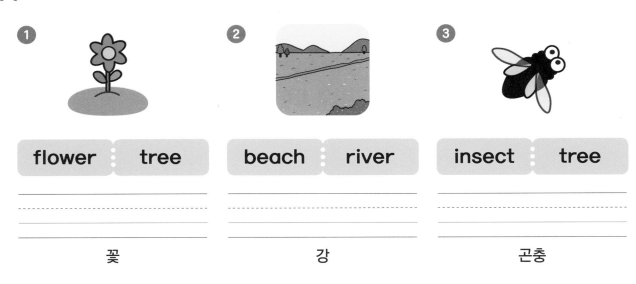

1 | flower | tree |

꽃

2 | beach | river |

강

3 | insect | tree |

곤충

B Find, circle, and write the words.

해변	beach
	beech
	baech

산	mountein
	mauntain
	mountain

심다, 식물	plant
	pleat
	prant

둘러싸다, 에워싸다	surraund
	surround
	surreund

C Connect and fill in the blanks.

 ①

 ②

 ③

Look at the beach.

_____을 보세요.

I climbed a mountain.

나는 _____을 올랐어요.

We plant tomatoes.

우리는 토마토를 _____.

D Choose and complete the sentences.

trees	insects	river

① 나는 강에서 수영했어요.

I swam in the _____.

② 우리는 나무를 심어요.

We plant _____.

③ 나는 날아다니는 곤충을 싫어해요.

I hate flying _____.

Check Up Read and check the words you don't know.

1차 복습

- ☐ flower
- ☐ tree
- ☐ river
- ☐ mountain
- ☐ beach
- ☐ insect
- ☐ surround
- ☐ plant

2차 복습

- ☐ rice
- ☐ honey
- ☐ empty
- ☐ flavor

3차 복습

- ☐ tall
- ☐ old
- ☐ beauty
- ☐ rude

※ 망각 제로! 1일 전 3일 전 7일 전 학습한 단어를 복습해요.

flower 꽃	tree 나무	river 강	mountain 산
beach 해변	insect 곤충	surround 둘러싸다, 에워싸다	plant 심다, 식물
rice 밥, 쌀	honey 꿀	empty 비어 있는, 빈	flavor 맛
tall 키가 큰	old 나이가 든, 낡은	beauty 아름다움	rude 무례한, 버릇없는

Sally's friends help her choose a gift.

PoP Quiz Choose and check the right words.

Rod suggests a cap as a gift.

로드는 선물로 _____를 제안해요.

- ☐ 모자
- ☐ 반지

Kiara thinks the gloves look nice.

키아라는 _____이 좋아 보인다고 생각해요.

- ☐ 장갑
- ☐ 넥타이

131

Catch Up

 **Listen, say, and color.**

Read & Write Write the **Basic Words** and **Jump Up Words**.

cap 모자	**I like this cap.** 나는 이 모자를 좋아해요.

ring 반지	**I gave her a ring.** 나는 그녀에게 반지를 주었어요.

tie 넥타이	**He wears a shirt and tie.** 그는 셔츠와 넥타이를 입어요.

gloves
장갑

I have gloves. (n)

나는 장갑을 가지고 있어요.

_____
- - - - - - - - - - - - - - - - -
_____

button
단추,
단추를 잠그다

I fastened the buttons. (n) (v)

나는 단추를 채웠어요.

_____
- - - - - - - - - - - - - - - - -
_____

exchange
교환하다

We exchanged **clothes.** (v)

우리는 옷을 교환했어요.

_____
- - - - - - - - - - - - - - - - -
_____

label
라벨, 상표

I remove the labels **from my clothes.** (n)

나는 옷의 라벨을 제거해요.

_____
- - - - - - - - - - - - - - - - -
_____

item
물품, 품목

She has a lot of luxury items. (n)

그녀는 비싼 물품들을 많이 가지고 있어요.

_____
- - - - - - - - - - - - - - - - -
_____

A Circle the letters and complete the words.

1

a e o u

c _ p
모자

2

m g z n

r i _ _
반지

3

l v g k

_ l o _ e s
장갑

B Connect and write the words.

1 exchange   •   • 단추,
단추를 잠그다   ....

2 button   •   • 교환하다   ....

3 label   •   • 물품, 품목   ....

4 item   •   • 라벨, 상표   ....

C Connect, choose, and complete the sentences.

| labels | exchanged | buttons |

1

우리는 옷을 교환했어요.

We _____ our clothes.

2

나는 단추를 채웠어요.

I fastened the _____.

3

나는 옷의 라벨을 제거해요.

I remove the _____ from my clothes.

D Circle the words and complete the sentences.

1 나는 장갑을 가지고 있어요.

| buttons | gloves |

I have _____.

2 그는 셔츠와 넥타이를 입어요.

| tie | ring |

He wears a shirt and _____.

Day 20 School Supplies

Check UP Read and check the words you don't know.

1차 복습

- [ ] cap
- [ ] ring
- [ ] tie
- [ ] gloves
- [ ] button
- [ ] exchange
- [ ] label
- [ ] item

2차 복습

- [ ] open
- [ ] close
- [ ] perform
- [ ] fasten

3차 복습

- [ ] afternoon
- [ ] beam
- [ ] gather
- [ ] silent

※ 망각 제로! 1일 전 3일 전 7일 전 학습한 단어를 복습해요.

Word Tip

cap 모자	**ring** 반지	**tie** 넥타이	**gloves** 장갑
button 단추, 단추를 잠그다	**exchange** 교환하다	**label** 라벨, 상표	**item** 물품, 품목
open 열다	**close** 닫다	**perform** 공연하다, 수행하다	**fasten** 매다, 고정시키다
afternoon 오후	**beam** 광선, 빛줄기	**gather** 모이다	**silent** 조용한

136

Whose desk is this?

PoP Quiz Choose and check the right words.

There is an eraser on the desk.

책상에 _____ 가 있어요.

- [ ] 필통
- [ ] 지우개

Mong thinks the desk is tidy.

몽은 책상이 _____ 생각해요.

- [ ] 깔끔한
- [ ] 물건

137

Catch Up

pencil
연필

I sharpened the pencil.
나는 연필을 깎았어요.

_____

_____

_____

eraser
지우개

Can I use your eraser?
지우개를 써도 될까요?

_____

_____

_____

glue
풀

She is using glue.
그녀는 풀을 사용하고 있어요.

_____

_____

_____

tape
테이프

He attached the photos with tape. (n)

그는 테이프로 사진들을 붙였어요.

---

calendar
달력

I'll mark the date on my calendar. (n)

제 달력에 날짜 표시해 놓을게요.

---

tidy
깔끔한,
잘 정돈된

I keep my locker tidy. (a)

나는 사물함을 깔끔하게 정리해요.

---

object
물건, 사물

We draw different objects in art class. (n)

우리는 미술 시간에 다른 물건을 그려요.

---

tools
도구, 연장

I need tools to fix my chair. (n)

나는 의자를 고칠 도구가 필요해요.

Skill Up

A Circle and trace the words.

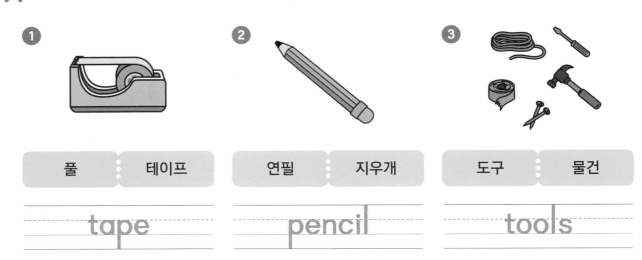

1
| 풀 | 테이프 |

tape

2
| 연필 | 지우개 |

pencil

3
| 도구 | 물건 |

tools

B Unscramble and write the words.

1 지우개   r e s r a e

2 풀   u g l e

3 물건, 사물   b j e t c o

4 깔끔한,
잘 정돈된   d i t y

140

C Connect and fill in the blanks.

1

I'll mark the date on my calendar.

제 _____에 날짜 표시해 놓을게요.

2

Can I use your eraser?

_____를 써도 될까요?

3

She is using glue.

그녀는 _____을 사용하고 있어요.

D Choose and complete the sentences.

pencil	tools	objects

1 나는 의자를 고칠 도구가 필요해요.

I need _____ to fix my chair.

2 우리는 미술 시간에 다른 물건을 그려요.

We draw different _____ in art class.

3 나는 연필을 깎았어요.

I sharpened the _____.

WORD SEARCH Find, circle, and write the words.

wringu

riceehoney

kopeniencloseo

flowerpriverhcap

pencilrieraserwo

ring

ICE CREAM

Day 16~20

rice 밥, 쌀	**honey** 꿀	**food** 음식	**bottle** 병	**cookie** 쿠키
complain 불평하다	**empty** 비어 있는, 빈	**flavor** 맛	**sit** 앉다	**stand** 일어서다
open 열다	**close** 닫다	**move** 옮기다, 움직이다	**attach** 붙이다	**perform** 공연하다, 수행하다
fasten 매다, 고정시키다	**flower** 꽃	**tree** 나무	**river** 강	**mountain** 산
beach 해변	**insect** 곤충	**surround** 둘러싸다, 에워싸다	**plant** 심다, 식물	**cap** 모자
ring 반지	**tie** 넥타이	**gloves** 장갑	**button** 단추, 단추를 잠그다	**exchange** 교환하다
label 라벨, 상표	**item** 물품, 품목	**pencil** 연필	**eraser** 지우개	**glue** 풀
tape 테이프	**calendar** 달력	**tidy** 깔끔한, 잘 정돈된	**object** 물건, 사물	**tools** 도구, 연장

맞힌 개수 : ☐ **/ 40**

❶ rice		㉑ 음식	
❷ honey		㉒ 병	
❸ empty		㉓ 쿠키	
❹ flavor		㉔ 불평하다	
❺ move		㉕ 열다	
❻ stand		㉖ 닫다	
❼ perform		㉗ 앉다	
❽ fasten		㉘ 붙이다	
❾ flower		㉙ 강	
❿ tree		㉚ 산	
⓫ surround		㉛ 해변	
⓬ plant		㉜ 곤충	
⓭ cap		㉝ 넥타이	
⓮ button		㉞ 장갑	
⓯ label		㉟ 반지	
⓰ item		㊱ 교환하다	
⓱ tidy		㊲ 풀	
⓲ pencil		㊳ 테이프	
⓳ object		㊴ 달력	
⓴ tools		㊵ 지우개	

Part 5

FINISH

START

Day 21 Body

Check Up Read and check the words you don't know.

1차 복습

- [ ] pencil
- [ ] eraser
- [ ] glue
- [ ] tape
- [ ] calendar
- [ ] tidy
- [ ] object
- [ ] tools

2차 복습

- [ ] river
- [ ] mountain
- [ ] beach
- [ ] plant

3차 복습

- [ ] business
- [ ] judge
- [ ] fair
- [ ] imagine

※ 망각 제로! 1일 전 3일 전 7일 전 학습한 단어를 복습해요.

pencil 연필	**eraser** 지우개	**glue** 풀	**tape** 테이프
calendar 달력	**tidy** 깔끔한, 잘 정돈된	**object** 물건, 사물	**tools** 도구, 연장
river 강	**mountain** 산	**beach** 해변	**plant** 심다, 식물
business 사업, 업무	**judge** 판사, 심판	**fair** 공평한, 공정한	**imagine** 상상하다

What's your favorite part of your body?

![Pop Quiz] **Choose and check the right words.**

Kiara has long arms.

키아라는 _____이 길어요.

☐ 팔

☐ 목

Sally likes her silky hair.

샐리는 자신의 찰랑이는 _____을 마음에 들어 해요.

☐ 머리카락

☐ 다리

Catch Up

Listen & Say   Listen, say, and color.

Read & Write   Write the **Basic Words** and **Jump Up Words**.

	n
neck 목	**She has a long neck.** 그녀는 긴 목을 가지고 있어요. _____

	n
hair 머리카락	**Her hair is short.** 그녀의 머리카락은 짧아요. _____

	n
arm 팔	**His arms have good muscle tone.** 그의 팔은 근육질이에요. _____

leg 다리	**I broke my leg.** 내 다리가 부러졌어요.	n

head 머리, 고개	**She touched my head.** 그녀는 내 머리를 만졌어요.	n

pain 통증, 고통	**She feels pain in her chest.** 그녀는 가슴에 통증을 느껴요.	n

pale 창백한	**You look pale.** 안색이 창백해 보여요.	a

comfort 위로, 위로하다	**I felt comfort in her arms.** 나는 그녀의 품에서 위로를 받았어요.	n v

Skill UP

A Circle and trace the words.

① 팔	다리	② 머리카락	머리	③ 팔	목

leg

head

neck

B Find, circle, and write the words.

팔	arn
	arm
	alm

머리카락	heir
	hear
	hair

통증, 고통	pain
	pein
	peen

창백한	pale
	pele
	peal

150

C Connect and fill in the blanks.

① I felt comfort in her arms.

나는 그녀의 품에서 ＿＿＿＿＿＿＿＿를 받았어요.

② She feels pain in her chest.

그녀는 가슴에 ＿＿＿＿＿＿＿＿을 느껴요.

③ You look pale.

안색이 ＿＿＿＿＿＿＿＿ 보여요.

D Circle the words and complete the sentences.

① 내 다리가 부러졌어요.

| leg | neck |

I broke my ＿＿＿＿＿＿.

② 그녀의 머리카락은 짧아요.

| hair | head |

Her ＿＿＿＿＿ is short.

Check UP Read and check the words you don't know.

1차 복습

- ☐ neck
- ☐ hair
- ☐ arm
- ☐ leg
- ☐ head
- ☐ pain
- ☐ pale
- ☐ comfort

2차 복습

- ☐ cap
- ☐ ring
- ☐ tie
- ☐ gloves

3차 복습

- ☐ food
- ☐ bottle
- ☐ cookie
- ☐ complain

※ **망각 제로!** 1일 전 3일 전 7일 전 학습한 단어를 복습해요.

 **Word Tip**

neck 목	hair 머리카락	arm 팔	leg 다리
head 머리, 고개	pain 통증, 고통	pale 창백한	comfort 위로, 위로하다
cap 모자	ring 반지	tie 넥타이	gloves 장갑
food 음식	bottle 병	cookie 쿠키	complain 불평하다

Let's go on a treasure hunt!

Pop Quiz Choose and check the right words.

They are searching for treasure.

그들은 보물을 _____요.

☐ 기대다

☐ 찾다

Sally found treasure in the bushes.

샐리는 수풀 _____ 보물을 찾았어요.

☐ 안에

☐ 아래에

Read &Write Write the **Basic Words** and **Jump Up Words**.

in ~ 안에	**The cat is in the box.** `prep` 고양이가 상자 안에 있어요.

on ~ 위에	**The book is on the desk.** `prep` 책이 책상 위에 있어요.

under ~ 아래에	**The book is under the desk.** `prep` 책이 책상 아래에 있어요.

up
위로

We walked up the hill. *prep*

우리는 언덕을 걸어 올라갔어요.

_____

down
아래로

We walked down the hill. *prep*

우리는 언덕을 걸어 내려갔어요.

_____

lean
기대다

He is leaning against a tree. *v*

그는 나무에 기대어 있어요.

_____

search
찾다, 뒤지다

I'm searching for my glasses. *v*

나는 안경을 찾고 있어요.

_____

rescue
구하다

They were rescued by helicopter. *v*

그들은 헬리콥터로 구조되었어요.

_____

Skill UP

A Circle and write the words.

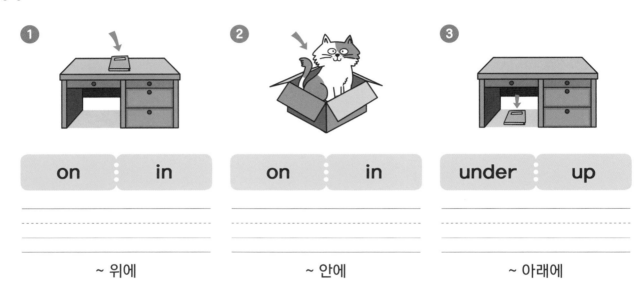

①
on	in

_____

~ 위에

②
on	in

_____

~ 안에

③
under	up

_____

~ 아래에

B Connect and write the words.

① up   •   • 구하다   _____

② lean   •   • 찾다, 뒤지다   _____

③ search   •   • 위로   _____

④ rescue   •   • 기대다   _____

C Connect, choose, and complete the sentences.

leaning   down   searching

1
우리는 언덕을 걸어 내려갔어요.

We walked _____ the hill.

2
그는 나무에 기대어 있어요.

He is _____ against a tree.

3
나는 안경을 찾고 있어요.

I'm _____ for my glasses.

D Choose and complete the sentences.

up   under   rescued

1 그들은 헬리콥터로 구조되었어요.

They were _____ by helicopter.

2 우리는 언덕을 걸어 올라갔어요.

We walked _____ the hill.

3 책이 책상 아래에 있어요.

The book is _____ the desk.

Day 23 Actions

Check Up Read and check the words you don't know.

1차 복습

- [ ] in
- [ ] on
- [ ] under
- [ ] up
- [ ] down
- [ ] lean
- [ ] search
- [ ] rescue

2차 복습

- [ ] calendar
- [ ] tidy
- [ ] object
- [ ] tools

3차 복습

- [ ] sit
- [ ] stand
- [ ] move
- [ ] attach

※ 망각 제로! 1일 전 3일 전 7일 전 학습한 단어를 복습해요.

Word Tip

in ~ 안에	**on** ~ 위에	**under** ~ 아래에	**up** 위로
down 아래로	**lean** 기대다	**search** 찾다, 뒤지다	**rescue** 구하다
calendar 달력	**tidy** 깔끔한, 잘 정돈된	**object** 물건, 사물	**tools** 도구, 연장
sit 앉다	**stand** 일어서다	**move** 옮기다, 움직이다	**attach** 붙이다

Dennis has good hearing.

Pop Quiz Choose and check the right words.

Rod and Sally are coming into the classroom.

로드와 샐리가 교실로 _____ 있어요.

- [ ] 보다
- [ ] 오다

Dennis heard their footsteps.

데니스는 그들의 발소리를 _____.

- [ ] 듣다
- [ ] 만나다

 Write the **Basic Words** and **Jump Up Words**.

go 가다	**I go to school.** 나는 학교에 가요.

come 오다	**I come home.** 나는 집에 와요.

see 보다	**I see a cat.** 나는 고양이를 봐요.

160

hear 듣다	**I hear some music.** ⓥ 나는 어떤 음악이 들려요.

meet 만나다	**I meet my friend.** ⓥ 나는 내 친구를 만나요.

celebrate 축하하다, 기념하다	**We celebrated his birthday.** ⓥ 우리는 그의 생일을 축하했어요.

whisper 속삭이다	**He whispered quietly.** ⓥ 그는 조용히 속삭였어요.

reach 닿다, ~에 이르다	**I wish I could reach the shelf.** ⓥ 나는 선반에 닿을 수 있으면 좋겠어요.

A Circle the letters and complete the words.

1

a o e y

c _ m _
오다

2

m g h t

_ e e _
만나다

3

a e i o

h _ _ r
듣다

B Connect and write the words.

1 see • • 닿다,
~에 이르다 _____

2 reach • • 보다 _____

3 whisper • • 축하하다,
기념하다 _____

4 celebrate • • 속삭이다 _____

C Connect and fill in the blanks.

1

I see a cat.

나는 고양이를 _____.

2

I go to school.

나는 학교에 _____.

3

I wish I could reach the shelf.

나는 선반에 _____ 수 있으면 좋겠어요.

D Circle the words and complete the sentences.

1 나는 어떤 음악이 들려요.

| see | hear |

I _____ some music.

2 나는 내 친구를 만나요.

| meet | come |

I _____ my friend.

Day 24 Describing Things & People

Check UP Read and check the words you don't know.

1차 복습

- [ ] go
- [ ] come
- [ ] see
- [ ] hear
- [ ] meet
- [ ] reach
- [ ] whisper
- [ ] celebrate

2차 복습

- [ ] arm
- [ ] leg
- [ ] pain
- [ ] pale

3차 복습

- [ ] flower
- [ ] tree
- [ ] insect
- [ ] surround

※ 망각 제로! 1일 전 3일 전 7일 전 학습한 단어를 복습해요.

Word Tip

go 가다	come 오다	see 보다	hear 듣다
meet 만나다	reach 닿다, ~에 이르다	whisper 속삭이다	celebrate 축하하다, 기념하다
arm 팔	leg 다리	pain 통증, 고통	pale 창백한
flower 꽃	tree 나무	insect 곤충	surround 둘러싸다, 에워싸다

Let me introduce my friends.

Kiara thinks Sally is curious.

키아라는 샐리가 _____ 생각해요.

☐ 새로운

☐ 호기심이 많은

Kiara thinks Dennis is odd sometimes.

키아라는 데니스가 가끔 _____ 생각해요.

☐ 진지한

☐ 이상한

165

Catch Up

 **Listen & Say** Listen, say, and color.

Read & Write Write the **Basic Words** and **Jump Up Words**.

new 새, 새로운	**The shoes are new.** ⓐ 신발이 새것이에요.

curious 호기심이 많은, 궁금한	**The kid is curious.** ⓐ 그 아이는 호기심이 많아요.

slow 느린	**The tortoise is slow.** ⓐ 거북이는 느려요.

166

bad
나쁜

The wolf is bad. ⓐ
늑대는 나빠요.

_____

good
좋은

I have a good idea. ⓐ
나는 좋은 생각이 있어요.

_____

odd
특이한, 이상한

It is an odd clock. ⓐ
그것은 특이한 시계예요.

_____

serious
진지한, 심각한

She looks serious. ⓐ
그녀는 진지해 보여요.

_____

eager
열심인, 열렬한

They are eager to learn. ⓐ
그들은 배우는 데 열심이에요.

_____

Skill UP

A Circle and trace the words.

1

좋은	나쁜

good

2

특이한	열심인

eager

3

느린	궁금한

slow

B Unscramble and write the words.

1 특이한, 이상한   d o d

2 진지한, 심각한   r i o s e s u

3 호기심이 많은, 궁금한   c i r u s o u

4 나쁜   d b a

C Connect, choose, and complete the sentences.

| curious | odd | serious |

1

그것은 특이한 시계예요.

It is an _____ clock.

2

그녀는 진지해 보여요.

She looks _____.

3

그 아이는 호기심이 많아요.

The kid is _____.

D Circle the words and complete the sentences.

1 신발은 새것이에요.

| new | good |

The shoes are _____.

2 그들은 배우는 데 열심이에요.

| eager | serious |

They are _____ to learn.

Day 25 Actions

1차 복습

- [ ] new
- [ ] bad
- [ ] slow
- [ ] curious
- [ ] good
- [ ] odd
- [ ] serious
- [ ] eager

2차 복습

- [ ] up
- [ ] down
- [ ] search
- [ ] rescue

3차 복습

- [ ] item
- [ ] exchange
- [ ] label
- [ ] button

※ **망각 제로!** 1일 전 3일 전 7일 전 학습한 단어를 복습해요.

Word Tip

new 새, 새로운 **bad** 나쁜 **slow** 느린 **curious** 호기심이 많은, 궁금한

good 좋은 **odd** 특이한, 이상한 **serious** 진지한, 심각한 **eager** 열심인, 열렬한

up 위로 **down** 아래로 **search** 찾다, 뒤지다 **rescue** 구하다

item 물품, 품목 **exchange** 교환하다 **label** 라벨, 상표 **button** 단추, 단추를 잠그다

Rod is in trouble.

POP Quiz Choose and check the right words.

They're playing at Rod's house.

그들은 로드의 집에서 _____ 있어요.

- [ ] 놀다
- [ ] 수영하다

Rod thinks his mom might scold him.

로드는 엄마가 그를 _____지도 모른다고 생각해요.

- [ ] 야단치다
- [ ] 시작하다

Catch Up

Listen & Say Listen, say, and color.

Read & Write Write the **Basic Words** and **Jump Up Words**.

---

start
시작하다

Let's start running.

달리기를 시작하자.

_____

---

stop
멈추다

We must stop at the red light.

우리는 빨간 불에 멈춰야 해요.

_____

---

swim
수영하다

I can swim.

나는 수영을 할 수 있어요.

_____

play
놀다

Let's play together.
같이 놀자.

_____
- - - - - - - - - - - - -
_____

ride
타다

Let's ride our bikes.
우리 자전거를 타자.

_____
- - - - - - - - - - - - -
_____

earn
(돈을) 벌다

I want to earn more money.
나는 돈을 더 벌고 싶어요.

_____
- - - - - - - - - - - - -
_____

accept
받아들이다

I accepted his offer.
나는 그의 제안을 받아들였어요.

_____
- - - - - - - - - - - - -
_____

scold
야단치다

Don't scold the puppy.
강아지를 야단치지 마세요.

_____
- - - - - - - - - - - - -
_____

A Circle the letters and complete the words.

①

p f l r

_ _ a y

놀다

②

c s k t

_ _ o l d

야단치다

③

a i e o

r _ d _

타다

B Connect and write the words.

① start · · 시작하다 _____

② swim · · (돈을) 벌다 _____

③ earn · · 수영하다 _____

④ accept · · 받아들이다 _____

C Connect and fill in the blanks.

1

I can swim.

나는 _____ 수 있어요.

2

We must stop at the red light.

우리는 빨간 불에 _____ 해요.

3

I want to earn more money.

나는 돈을 더 _____ 싶어요.

D Choose and complete the sentences.

start	scold	ride

1 우리 자전거를 타자.

Let's _____ our bikes.

2 강아지를 야단치지 마세요.

Don't _____ the puppy.

3 달리기를 시작하자.

Let's _____ running.

175

WORD PUZZLE Complete the word puzzle.

ACROSS

② She has a long _____ .

⑥ The book is _____ the desk.

⑦ I _____ some music.

⑧ I have a _____ idea.

⑨ Let's _____ running.

DOWN

① I _____ a cat.

③ The kid is _____ .

④ The cat is _____ the box.

⑤ Let's _____ together.

⑦ Her _____ is short.

neck 목	**hair** 머리카락	**arm** 팔	**leg** 다리	**head** 머리, 고개
pain 통증, 고통	**pale** 창백한	**comfort** 위로, 위로하다	**in** ~ 안에	**on** ~ 위에
under ~ 아래에	**up** 위로	**down** 아래로	**lean** 기대다	**search** 찾다, 뒤지다
rescue 구하다	**go** 가다	**come** 오다	**see** 보다	**hear** 듣다
meet 만나다	**celebrate** 축하하다, 기념하다	**whisper** 속삭이다	**reach** 닿다, ~에 이르다	**new** 새, 새로운
curious 호기심이 많은, 궁금한	**slow** 느린	**bad** 나쁜	**good** 좋은	**odd** 특이한, 이상한
serious 진지한, 심각한	**eager** 열심인, 열렬한	**start** 시작하다	**stop** 멈추다	**swim** 수영하다
play 놀다	**ride** 타다	**earn** (돈을) 벌다	**accept** 받아들이다	**scold** 야단치다

Day
21~25

맞힌 개수 : [ ] / 40

① neck		㉑ 팔	
② hair		㉒ 다리	
③ pale		㉓ 머리, 고개	
④ comfort		㉔ 통증, 고통	
⑤ in		㉕ ~ 아래에	
⑥ on		㉖ 위로	
⑦ search		㉗ 아래로	
⑧ rescue		㉘ 기대다	
⑨ go		㉙ 보다	
⑩ come		㉚ 듣다	
⑪ celebrate		㉛ 만나다	
⑫ reach		㉜ 속삭이다	
⑬ odd		㉝ 느린	
⑭ curious		㉞ 나쁜	
⑮ serious		㉟ 좋은	
⑯ eager		㊱ 새, 새로운	
⑰ start		㊲ 수영하다	
⑱ stop		㊳ 놀다	
⑲ accept		㊴ 타다	
⑳ scold		㊵ (돈을) 벌다	

Answer Key

Level 1.1

Day 01

P11

POP Quiz ☐ 행복한 ✓ 슬픈 ✓ 두려워하는 ☐ 화가 난

P14~15

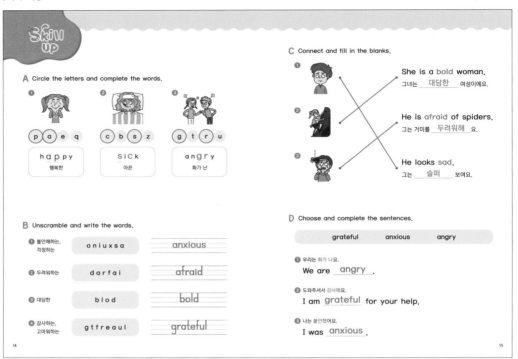

Day 02

P17

POP Quiz ☐ 남동생 ✓ 여동생 ✓ 오빠 ☐ 언니

P20~21

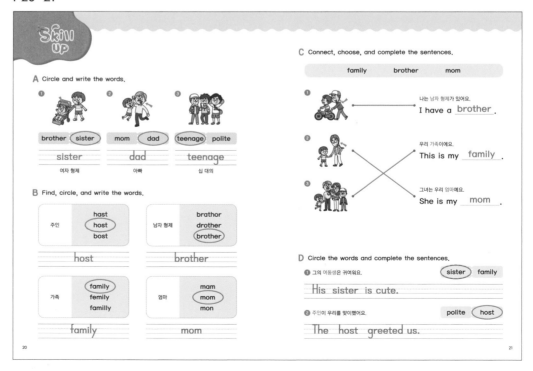

Day 03

 **Pop Quiz** ☐ 강아지 ☑ 고양이 ☑ 오리 ☐ 새

P26~27

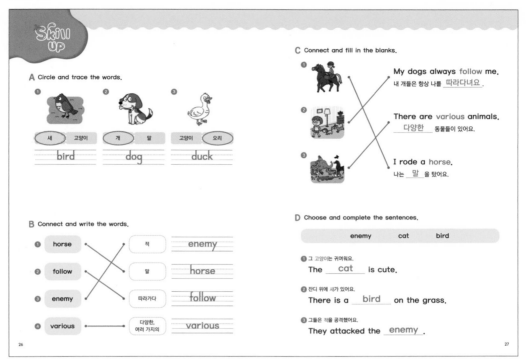

Skill up

A Circle and trace the words.

❶ (새) 고양이   bird
❷ (개) 말   dog
❸ 고양이 (오리)   duck

B Connect and write the words.

❶ horse — 적 — enemy
❷ follow — 말 — horse
❸ enemy — 따라가다 — follow
❹ various — 다양한, 여러 가지의 — various

C Connect and fill in the blanks.

❶ My dogs always follow me.
내 개들은 항상 나를 <u>따라다녀요</u> .

❷ There are various animals.
<u>다양한</u> 동물들이 있어요.

❸ I rode a horse.
나는 <u>말</u> 을 탔어요.

D Choose and complete the sentences.

    enemy   cat   bird

❶ 그 고양이는 귀여워요.
The <u>cat</u> is cute.

❷ 잔디 위에 새가 있어요.
There is a <u>bird</u> on the grass.

❸ 그들은 적을 공격했어요.
They attacked the <u>enemy</u> .

26   27

Day 04

 **Pop Quiz** ☑ 걷다 ☐ 춤추다 ☐ 노래하다 ☑ 달리다, 뛰다

P32~33

Skill up

A Circle the letters and complete the words.

❶ (a) u (e) i   r u n   달리다, 뛰다
❷ (a) b z (g)   a r g u e   다투다, 언쟁하다
❸ f (g) (r) u   f r o w n   눈살을 찌푸리다

B Unscramble and write the words.

❶ 걷다   a k l w   walk
❷ 부르다, 전화하다   l a c l   call
❸ 춤추다   e d a c n   dance
❹ 벗다, 치우다   e r v o e m   remove

C Connect, choose, and complete the sentences.

    walk   sing   dances

❶ 그들은 노래하는 것을 좋아해요.
They like to <u>sing</u> .

❷ 나는 학교에 걸어가요.
I <u>walk</u> to school.

❸ 그는 엄마와 춤춰요.
He <u>dances</u> with his mom.

D Circle the words and complete the sentences.

❶ 나는 친구와 다퉜어요.   (argued) frowned
<u>I argued with my friend.</u>

❷ 아빠가 재킷을 벗어요.   runs (removes)
<u>Dad removes his jacket.</u>

32   33

P35

Pop Quiz ✓ 코 ☐ 입 ☐ 귀 ✓ 눈

P38~39

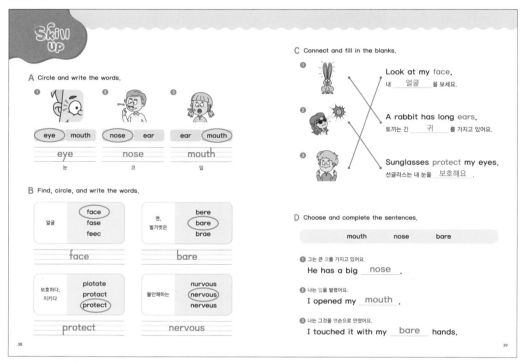

P40   P42

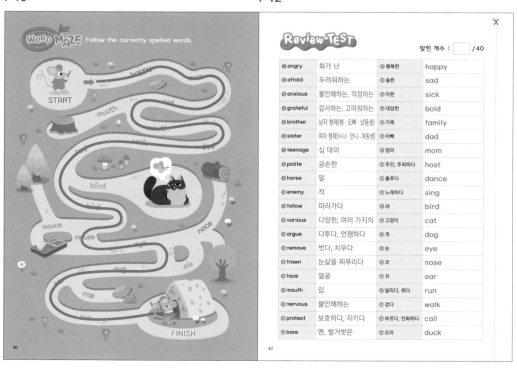

Day 06

P45

Pop Quiz  노란색(의) ✓ 빨간색(의) ✓ 파란색(의) 초록색(의)

P48~49

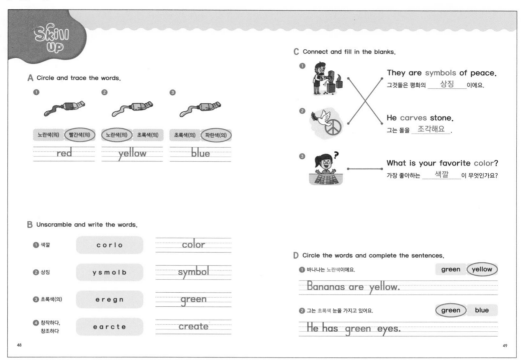

Skill UP

A Circle and trace the words.

❶ 노란색(의) (빨간색(의)) — red
❷ (노란색(의)) 초록색(의) — yellow
❸ 초록색(의) (파란색(의)) — blue

B Unscramble and write the words.

❶ 색깔 — c o r l o — color
❷ 상징 — y s m o l b — symbol
❸ 초록색(의) — e r e g n — green
❹ 창작하다, 창조하다 — e a r c t e — create

C Connect and fill in the blanks.

❶ They are symbols of peace.
그것들은 평화의 ___상징___ 이에요.

❷ He carves stone.
그는 돌을 ___조각해요___ .

❸ What is your favorite color?
가장 좋아하는 ___색깔___ 이 무엇인가요?

D Circle the words and complete the sentences.

❶ 바나나는 노란색이에요. green (yellow)
Bananas are yellow.

❷ 그는 초록색 눈을 가지고 있어요. (green) blue
He has green eyes.

48   49

Day 07

P51

Pop Quiz ✓ 책상 열쇠 ✓ 침대 방

P54~55

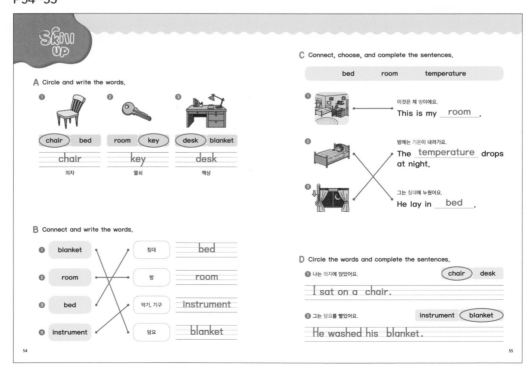

Skill UP

A Circle and write the words.

❶ (chair) bed — chair — 의자
❷ room (key) — key — 열쇠
❸ (desk) blanket — desk — 책상

B Connect and write the words.

❶ blanket — 침대 — bed
❷ room — 방 — room
❸ bed — 악기, 기구 — instrument
❹ instrument — 담요 — blanket

C Connect, choose, and complete the sentences.

bed   room   temperature

❶ 이것은 제 방이에요.
This is my ___room___ .

❷ 밤에는 기온이 내려가요.
The ___temperature___ drops at night.

❸ 그는 침대에 누워어요.
He lay in ___bed___ .

D Circle the words and complete the sentences.

❶ 나는 의자에 앉았어요. (chair) desk
I sat on a chair.

❷ 그는 담요를 빨았어요. instrument (blanket)
He washed his blanket.

54   55

Day 08

P57

 동물원 ✓ 사나운 ✓ 날카로운 기린

P60~61

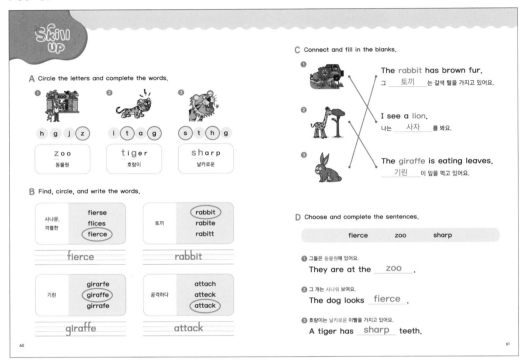

A Circle the letters and complete the words.

① h g j (z) → z o o / 동물원
② i (t) a (g) → t i g e r / 호랑이
③ s (t) (h) g → s h a r p / 날카로운

B Find, circle, and write the words.

사나운, 격렬한 | fierse / flices / (fierce) → fierce
토끼 | (rabbit) / rabite / rabitt → rabbit
기린 | girarfe / (giraffe) / girrafe → giraffe
공격하다 | attach / atteck / (attack) → attack

C Connect and fill in the blanks.

① The rabbit has brown fur.
그 __토끼__ 는 갈색 털을 가지고 있어요.

② I see a lion.
나는 __사자__ 를 봐요.

③ The giraffe is eating leaves.
__기린__ 이 잎을 먹고 있어요.

D Choose and complete the sentences.

fierce   zoo   sharp

① 그들은 동물원에 있어요.
They are at the __zoo__.

② 그 개는 사나워 보여요.
The dog looks __fierce__.

③ 호랑이는 날카로운 이빨을 가지고 있어요.
A tiger has __sharp__ teeth.

60 / 61

Day 09

P63

 큰 ✓ 작은 짧은 ✓ 긴

P66~67

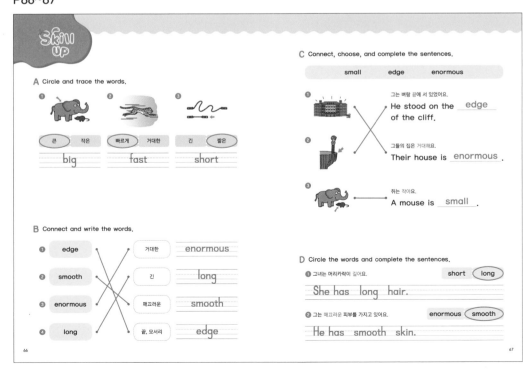

A Circle and trace the words.

① (큰) 작은 → big
② 빠르게 (거대한) → fast
③ (긴) 짧은 → short

B Connect and write the words.

① edge — 끝, 모서리 → edge
② smooth — 매끄러운 → smooth
③ enormous — 거대한 → enormous
④ long — 긴 → long

C Connect, choose, and complete the sentences.

small   edge   enormous

① 그는 벼랑 끝에 서 있었어요.
He stood on the __edge__ of the cliff.

② 그들의 집은 거대해요.
Their house is __enormous__.

③ 쥐는 작아요.
A mouse is __small__.

D Circle the words and complete the sentences.

① 그녀는 머리카락이 길어요.   short (long)
She has long hair.

② 그는 매끄러운 피부를 가지고 있어요.   enormous (smooth)
He has smooth skin.

66 / 67

P69

POP Quiz ✓빵 ☐고기 ✓달걀 ☐생선

P72~73

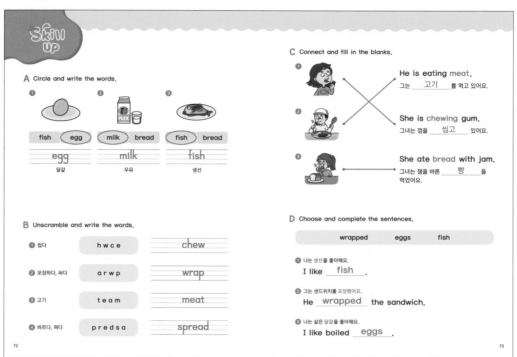

Skill UP

A Circle and write the words.

① (egg) — egg 달걀
② (milk) — milk 우유
③ (fish) — fish 생선

B Unscramble and write the words.

① 씹다　h w c e　→ chew
② 포장하다, 싸다　a r w p　→ wrap
③ 고기　t e a m　→ meat
④ 바르다, 펴다　p r e d s a　→ spread

C Connect and fill in the blanks.

① He is eating meat.
그는 __고기__ 를 먹고 있어요.

② She is chewing gum.
그녀는 껌을 __씹고__ 있어요.

③ She ate bread with jam.
그녀는 잼을 바른 __빵__ 을 먹었어요.

D Choose and complete the sentences.

wrapped　eggs　fish

① 나는 생선을 좋아해요.
I like __fish__ .

② 그는 샌드위치를 포장했어요.
He __wrapped__ the sandwich.

③ 나는 삶은 달걀을 좋아해요.
I like boiled __eggs__ .

72　73

P74

WORD COLORING Color the correctly spelled words.
Then write the answer.

ifsh　raod　leng
desk　big　tigar
long　beed
tiger
ricee　red
giraffe　yellew
deks　llion　bede
chair　deask
meat　yellow
meeat　egg
short　gireffe
bulee　fish　blue　lion　bed
bread
shork　tijer　chairr　liion

Q. What animal do you see? [rabbit]

74

P76

Review TEST　맞힌 개수 : ☐ / 40

① red	빨간색(의)	㉑ 초록색(의)	green
② yellow	노란색(의)	㉒ 파란색(의)	blue
③ symbol	상징	㉓ 색깔	color
④ create	창작하다, 창조하다	㉔ 조각하다	carve
⑤ bed	침대	㉕ 책상	desk
⑥ chair	의자	㉖ 열쇠	key
⑦ temperature	온도	㉗ 방	room
⑧ blanket	담요	㉘ 악기, 기구	instrument
⑨ zoo	동물원	㉙ 호랑이	tiger
⑩ lion	사자	㉚ 토끼	rabbit
⑪ fierce	사나운, 격렬한	㉛ 기린	giraffe
⑫ attack	공격하다	㉜ 날카로운	sharp
⑬ big	큰	㉝ 빠르게, 빠른	fast
⑭ small	작은	㉞ 긴	long
⑮ enormous	거대한	㉟ 짧은	short
⑯ smooth	매끄러운	㊱ 끝, 모서리	edge
⑰ fish	생선	㊲ 빵	bread
⑱ meat	고기	㊳ 달걀	egg
⑲ spread	바르다, 펴다	㊴ 우유	milk
⑳ chew	씹다	㊵ 포장하다, 싸다	wrap

76

Day 11

Pop Quiz  ✓ 사람들 ☐ 아기 ☐ 또래 ✓ 사람

P82~83

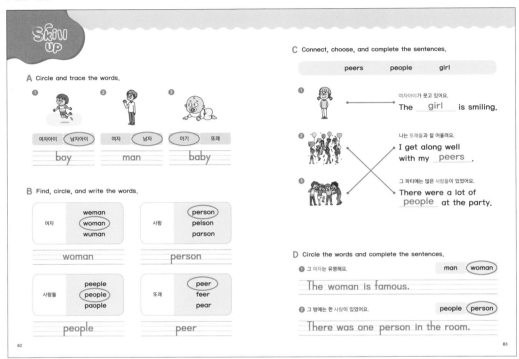

Skill Up

A Circle and trace the words.

① (남자아이) / 여자아이 — boy
② (남자) / 여자 — man
③ (아기) / 또래 — baby

B Find, circle, and write the words.

여자: weman / (woman) / wuman → woman
사람: (person) / pelson / parson → person
사람들: peeple / (people) / paople → people
또래: (peer) / feer / pear → peer

C Connect, choose, and complete the sentences.

| peers | people | girl |

① 여자아이가 웃고 있어요.
The **girl** is smiling.

② 나는 또래들과 잘 어울려요.
I get along well with my **peers**.

③ 그 파티에는 많은 사람들이 있었어요.
There were a lot of **people** at the party.

D Circle the words and complete the sentences.

① 그 여자는 유명해요. man / (woman)
The woman is famous.

② 그 방에는 한 사람이 있었어요. people / (person)
There was one person in the room.

82   83

Day 12

Pop Quiz ☐ 달 ✓ 하늘 ✓ 빤히 쳐다보다 ☐ 날이 밝다

P88~89

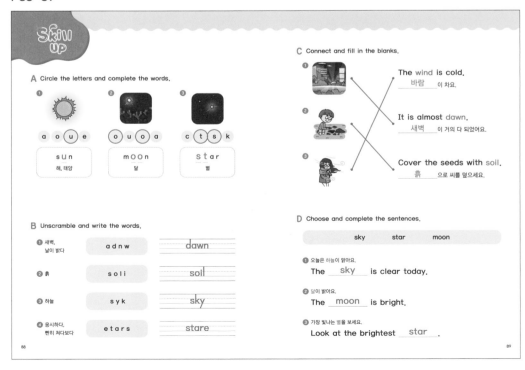

Skill Up

A Circle the letters and complete the words.

① a (o) (u) e → s u n / 해, 태양
② (o) u (o) a → m o o n / 달
③ c (t) (s) k → s t a r / 별

B Unscramble and write the words.

① 새벽, 날이 밝다 — a d n w → dawn
② 흙 — s o l i → soil
③ 하늘 — s y k → sky
④ 응시하다, 빤히 쳐다보다 — e t a r s → stare

C Connect and fill in the blanks.

① The wind is cold.
바람 이 차요.

② It is almost dawn.
새벽 이 거의 다 되었어요.

③ Cover the seeds with soil.
흙 으로 씨를 덮으세요.

D Choose and complete the sentences.

| sky | star | moon |

① 오늘은 하늘이 맑아요.
The **sky** is clear today.

② 달이 밝아요.
The **moon** is bright.

③ 가장 빛나는 별을 보세요.
Look at the brightest **star**.

88   89

Day 13

P91

 ✓ 예쁜 ☐ 어린 ✓ 키가 큰 ☐ 키가 작은

P94~95

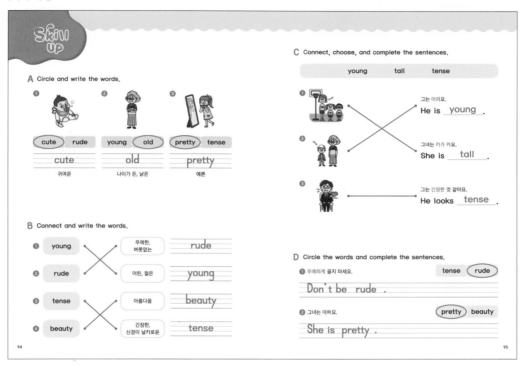

Skill Up

A Circle and write the words.

❶ (cute) rude
cute
귀여운

❷ young (old)
old
나이가 든, 낡은

❸ (pretty) tense
pretty
예쁜

B Connect and write the words.

❶ young — 무례한, 버릇없는 — rude
❷ rude — 어린, 젊은 — young
❸ tense — 아름다운 — beauty
❹ beauty — 긴장한, 신경이 날카로운 — tense

C Connect, choose, and complete the sentences.

young   tall   tense

❶ 그는 어려요.
He is __young__ .

❷ 그녀는 키가 커요.
She is __tall__ .

❸ 그는 긴장한 것 같아요.
He looks __tense__ .

D Circle the words and complete the sentences.

❶ 무례하게 굴지 마세요.   tense (rude)
Don't be rude .

❷ 그녀는 예뻐요.   (pretty) beauty
She is pretty .

94
95

Day 14

P97

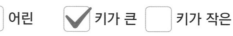 ✓ 아침 ☐ 저녁 ☐ 밤 ✓ 오후

P100~101

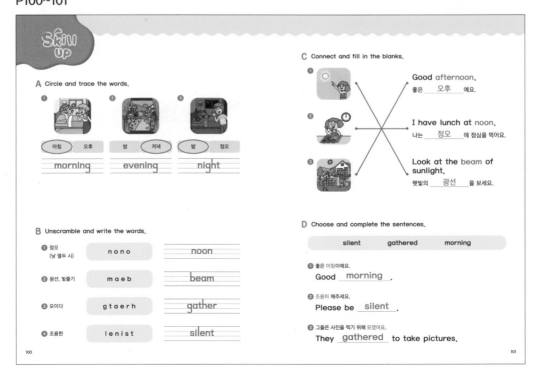

Skill Up

A Circle and trace the words.

❶ (아침) 오후
morning

❷ 밤 (저녁)
evening

❸ (밤) 정오
night

B Unscramble and write the words.

❶ 정오 (낮 열두 시)   n o n o   noon

❷ 광선, 빛줄기   m a e b   beam

❸ 모이다   g t a e r h   gather

❹ 조용한   l e n i s t   silent

C Connect and fill in the blanks.

❶ Good afternoon.
좋은 __오후__ 예요.

❷ I have lunch at noon.
나는 __정오__ 에 점심을 먹어요.

❸ Look at the beam of sunlight.
햇빛의 __광선__ 을 보세요.

D Choose and complete the sentences.

silent   gathered   morning

❶ 좋은 아침이에요.
Good __morning__ .

❷ 조용히 해주세요.
Please be __silent__ .

❸ 그들은 사진을 찍기 위해 모였어요.
They __gathered__ to take pictures.

100
101

Day 15

P103

POP Quiz ✓ 상상하다 ☐ 심판하다 ☐ 간호사 ✓ 의사

P106~107

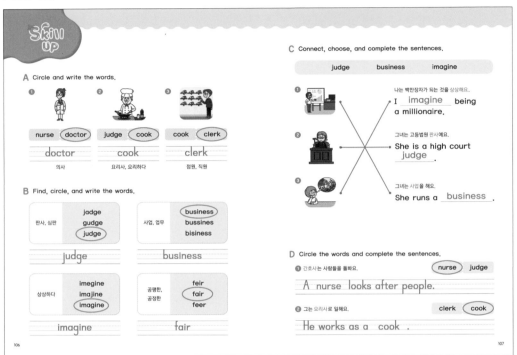

Day 11~15

P108

P110

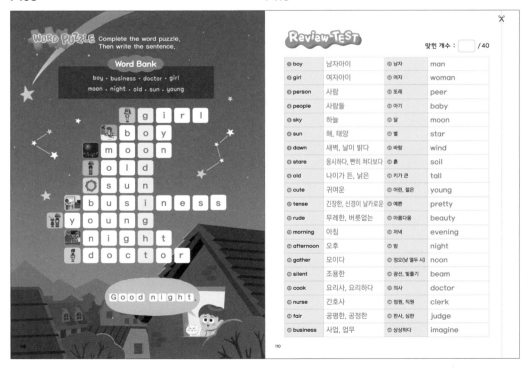

Day 16

P113

 **Pop Quiz** ☑ 꿀 ☐ 음식 ☑ 비어 있는 ☐ 불평하는

P116~117

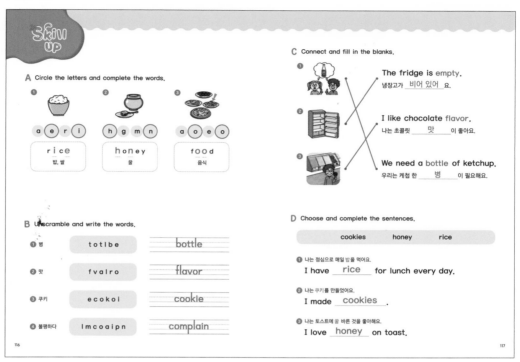

Skill UP

A Circle the letters and complete the words.

❶ a (e) (r) (i) → r i c e 밥, 쌀

❷ (h) g m (n) → h o n e y 꿀

❸ (a) (o) (e) (o) → f o o d 음식

B Unscramble and write the words.

❶ 병 totlbe bottle

❷ 맛 fvalro flavor

❸ 쿠키 ecokoi cookie

❹ 불평하다 lmcoaipn complain

C Connect and fill in the blanks.

❶ **The fridge is empty.** 냉장고가 비어 있어 요.

❷ **I like chocolate flavor.** 나는 초콜릿 맛 이 좋아요.

❸ **We need a bottle of ketchup.** 우리는 케첩 한 병 이 필요해요.

D Choose and complete the sentences.

cookies   honey   rice

❶ 나는 점심으로 매일 밥을 먹어요. I have rice for lunch every day.

❷ 나는 쿠키를 만들었어요. I made cookies .

❸ 나는 토스트에 꿀 바른 것을 좋아해요. I love honey on toast.

116   117

Day 17

P119

 **Pop Quiz** ☐ 닫다 ☑ 열다 ☑ 매다 ☐ 붙이다

P122~123

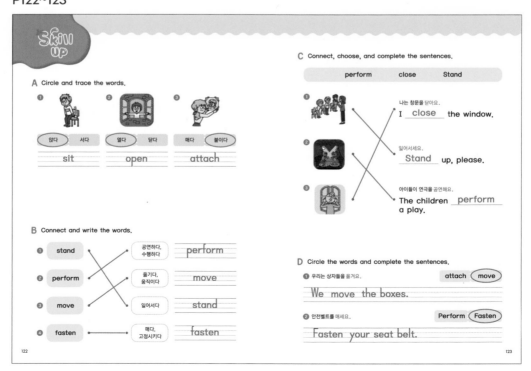

Skill UP

A Circle and trace the words.

❶ (앉다) 서다 sit

❷ 열다 (닫다) open

❸ 매다 (붙이다) attach

B Connect and write the words.

❶ stand — 공연하다, 수행하다 perform

❷ perform — 옮기다, 움직이다 move

❸ move — 일어서다 stand

❹ fasten — 매다, 고정시키다 fasten

C Connect, choose, and complete the sentences.

perform   close   Stand

❶ 나는 창문을 닫아요. I close the window.

❷ 일어서세요. Stand up, please.

❸ 아이들이 연극을 공연해요. The children perform a play.

D Circle the words and complete the sentences.

❶ 우리는 상자들을 옮겨요.   attach (move) We move the boxes.

❷ 안전벨트를 매세요.   Perform (Fasten) Fasten your seat belt.

122   123

Day 18

P125

Pop Quiz ☐ 산 ☑ 꽃 ☑ 나무 ☐ 해변

P128~129

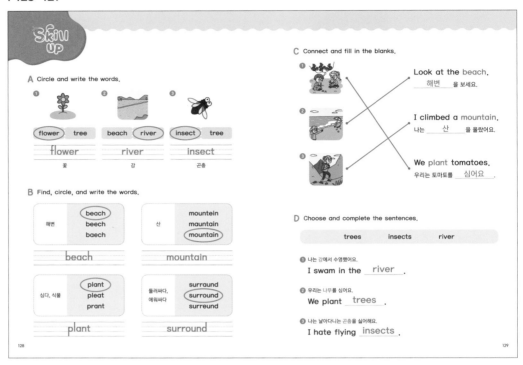

Skill UP

A Circle and write the words.

1. **flower** / tree → flower (꽃)
2. beach / **river** → river (강)
3. **insect** / tree → insect (곤충)

B Find, circle, and write the words.

해변: **beach** / beech / baech → beach

산: mountein / mauntain / **mountain** → mountain

심다, 식물: **plant** / pleat / prant → plant

둘러싸다, 에워싸다: **surround** / surrond / surreund → surround

C Connect and fill in the blanks.

1. Look at the beach.
   해변 을 보세요.

2. I climbed a mountain.
   나는 산 을 올랐어요.

3. We plant tomatoes.
   우리는 토마토를 심어요.

D Choose and complete the sentences.

trees insects river

1. 나는 강에서 수영했어요.
   I swam in the river.

2. 우리는 나무를 심어요.
   We plant trees.

3. 나는 날아다니는 곤충을 싫어해요.
   I hate flying insects.

128   129

Day 19

P131

Pop Quiz ☑ 모자 ☐ 반지 ☑ 장갑 ☐ 넥타이

P134~135

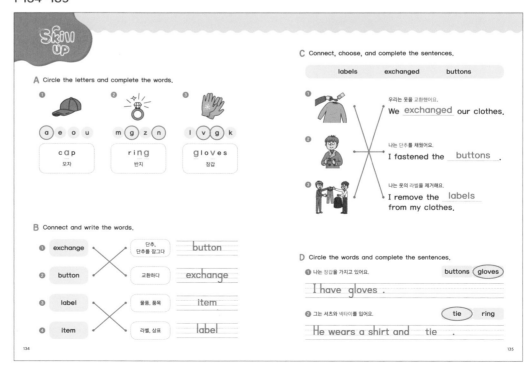

Skill UP

A Circle the letters and complete the words.

1. a **e** o u → c a p (모자)
2. m **g** z **n** → r i n g (반지)
3. l **v** g k → g l o v e s (장갑)

B Connect and write the words.

1. exchange — 단추, 단추를 잠그다 → button
2. button — 교환하다 → exchange
3. label — 물품, 품목 → item
4. item — 라벨, 상표 → label

C Connect, choose, and complete the sentences.

labels exchanged buttons

1. 우리는 옷을 교환했어요.
   We exchanged our clothes.

2. 나는 단추를 채웠어요.
   I fastened the buttons.

3. 나는 옷의 라벨을 제거해요.
   I remove the labels from my clothes.

D Circle the words and complete the sentences.

1. 나는 장갑을 가지고 있어요. buttons **gloves**
   I have gloves.

2. 그는 셔츠와 넥타이를 입어요. **tie** ring
   He wears a shirt and tie.

134   135

Day 20

P137

 **Pop Quiz** ☐ 필통 ☑ 지우개 ☑ 깔끔한 ☐ 물건

P140~141

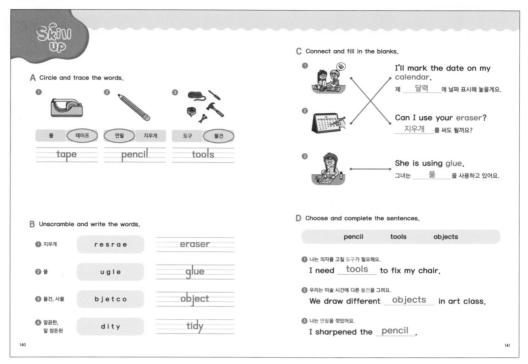

A Circle and trace the words.

① 풀 (테이프) → tape
② 연필 (지우개) → pencil
③ 도구 (물건) → tools

B Unscramble and write the words.

① 지우개 r e s r a e → eraser
② 풀 u g l e → glue
③ 물건, 사물 b j e t c o → object
④ 깔끔한, 잘 정돈된 d i t y → tidy

C Connect and fill in the blanks.

① I'll mark the date on my calendar.
제 __달력__ 에 날짜 표시해 놓을게요.

② Can I use your eraser?
__지우개__ 를 써도 될까요?

③ She is using glue.
그녀는 __풀__ 을 사용하고 있어요.

D Choose and complete the sentences.

pencil tools objects

① 나는 의자를 고칠 도구가 필요해요.
I need __tools__ to fix my chair.

② 우리는 미술 시간에 다른 물건을 그려요.
We draw different __objects__ in art class.

③ 나는 연필을 깎았어요.
I sharpened the __pencil__ .

140   141

Day 16~20

P142

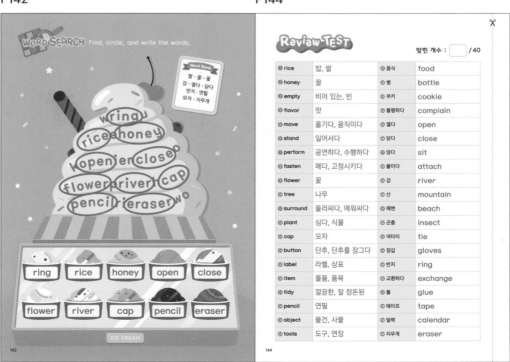

WORD SEARCH Find, circle, and write the words.

Word Bank
쌀 · 꿀 · 꽃
강 · 열다 · 닫다
반지 · 연필
모자 · 지우개

wringu
rice honey
kopenjerclose
flower river cap
pencil eraser wo

ring rice honey open close
flower river cap pencil eraser

ICE CREAM

142

P144

Review TEST   맞힌 개수 : ☐ / 40

① rice	밥, 쌀	㉑ 음식	food
② honey	꿀	㉒ 병	bottle
③ empty	비어 있는, 빈	㉓ 쿠키	cookie
④ flavor	맛	㉔ 불평하다	complain
⑤ move	옮기다, 움직이다	㉕ 열다	open
⑥ stand	일어서다	㉖ 닫다	close
⑦ perform	공연하다, 수행하다	㉗ 앉다	sit
⑧ fasten	매다, 고정시키다	㉘ 붙이다	attach
⑨ flower	꽃	㉙ 강	river
⑩ tree	나무	㉚ 산	mountain
⑪ surround	둘러싸다, 에워싸다	㉛ 해변	beach
⑫ plant	심다, 식물	㉜ 곤충	insect
⑬ cap	모자	㉝ 넥타이	tie
⑭ button	단추, 단추를 잠그다	㉞ 장갑	gloves
⑮ label	라벨, 상표	㉟ 반지	ring
⑯ item	물품, 품목	㊱ 교환하다	exchange
⑰ tidy	깔끔한, 잘 정돈된	㊲ 풀	glue
⑱ pencil	연필	㊳ 테이프	tape
⑲ object	물건, 사물	㊴ 달력	calendar
⑳ tools	도구, 연장	㊵ 지우개	eraser

144

Day 21

P147

Pop Quiz  ✓팔 □목  ✓머리카락 □다리

P150~151

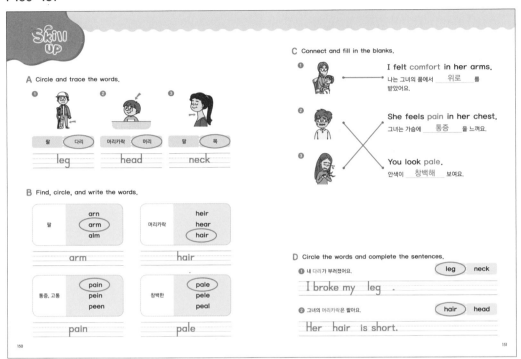

Skill Up

A Circle and trace the words.

① 팔 (다리) — leg
② 머리카락 (머리) — head
③ 팔 (목) — neck

B Find, circle, and write the words.

팔 — arn / (arm) / alm — arm
머리카락 — heir / hear / (hair) — hair
통증, 고통 — (pain) / pein / peen — pain
창백한 — (pale) / pele / peal — pale

C Connect and fill in the blanks.

① I felt comfort in her arms.
나는 그녀의 품에서 ___위로___ 를 받았어요.

② She feels pain in her chest.
그녀는 가슴에 ___통증___ 을 느껴요.

③ You look pale.
안색이 ___창백해___ 보여요.

D Circle the words and complete the sentences.

① 내 다리가 부러졌어요. (leg) neck
I broke my leg .

② 그녀의 머리카락은 짧아요. (hair) head
Her hair is short.

150 / 151

Day 22

P153

Pop Quiz □기대다 ✓찾다  ✓안에 □아래에

P156~157

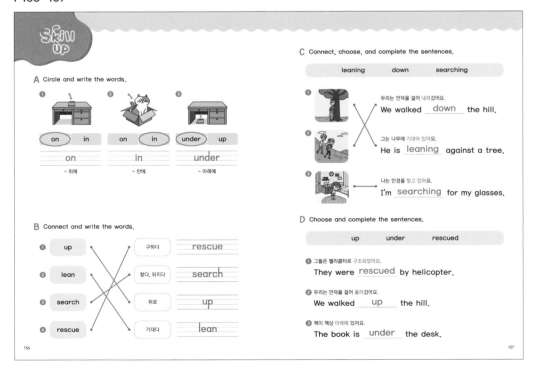

Skill Up

A Circle and write the words.

① (on) in — on — ~ 위에
② on (in) — in — ~ 안에
③ (under) up — under — ~ 아래에

B Connect and write the words.

① up — 구하다 — rescue
② lean — 찾다, 뒤지다 — search
③ search — 위로 — up
④ rescue — 기대다 — lean

C Connect, choose, and complete the sentences.

leaning   down   searching

① 우리는 언덕을 걸어 내려갔어요.
We walked __down__ the hill.

② 그는 나무에 기대어 있어요.
He is leaning against a tree.

③ 나는 안경을 찾고 있어요.
I'm searching for my glasses.

D Choose and complete the sentences.

up   under   rescued

① 그들은 헬리콥터로 구조되었어요.
They were rescued by helicopter.

② 우리는 언덕을 걸어 올라갔어요.
We walked __up__ the hill.

③ 책이 책상 아래에 있어요.
The book is under the desk.

156 / 157

Day 23

P159

Pop Quiz ☐ 보다 ☑ 오다 ☑ 듣다 ☐ 만나다

P162~163

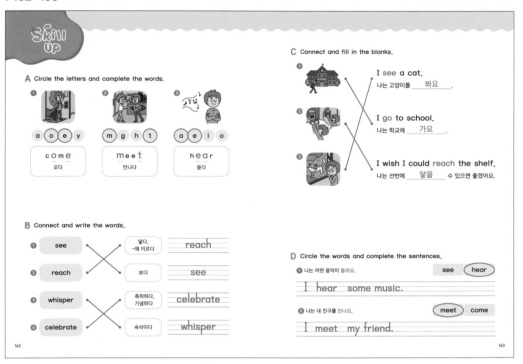

Skill Up

A Circle the letters and complete the words.

① a (o) e y → c o m e — 오다

② (m) g h (t) → m e e t — 만나다

③ a (e) i o → h e a r — 듣다

B Connect and write the words.

① see — 달다, -에 이르다 — reach
② reach — 보다 — see
③ whisper — 축하하다, 기념하다 — celebrate
④ celebrate — 속삭이다 — whisper

C Connect and fill in the blanks.

① I see a cat. 나는 고양이를 __봐요__.

② I go to school. 나는 학교에 __가요__.

③ I wish I could reach the shelf. 나는 선반에 __닿을__ 수 있으면 좋겠어요.

D Circle the words and complete the sentences.

① 나는 어떤 음악이 들려요.   see / (hear)
I __hear__ some music.

② 나는 내 친구를 만나요.   (meet) / come
I __meet__ my friend.

162 163

Day 24

P165

Pop Quiz ☐ 새로운 ☑ 호기심이 많은 ☐ 진지한 ☑ 이상한

P168~169

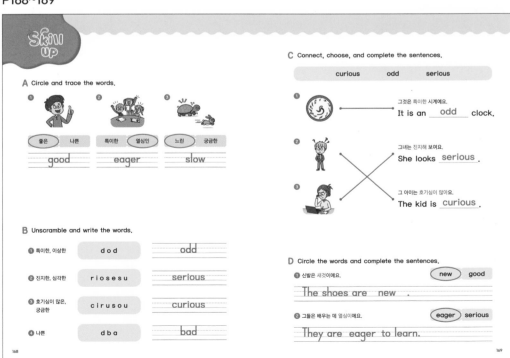

Skill Up

A Circle and trace the words.

① (좋은) 나쁜 — good
② 특이한 (열심인) — eager
③ (느린) 궁금한 — slow

B Unscramble and write the words.

① 특이한, 이상한   d o d → odd
② 진지한, 심각한   r i o s e s u → serious
③ 호기심이 많은, 궁금한   c i r u s o u → curious
④ 나쁜   d b a → bad

C Connect, choose, and complete the sentences.

curious   odd   serious

① 그것은 특이한 시계예요. It is an __odd__ clock.

② 그녀는 진지해 보여요. She looks __serious__.

③ 그 아이는 호기심이 많아요. The kid is __curious__.

D Circle the words and complete the sentences.

① 신발은 새것이에요.   (new) good
The shoes are __new__.

② 그들은 배우는 데 열심이에요.   (eager) serious
They are __eager__ to learn.

168 169

P171

☑ 놀다 ☐ 수영하다 ☑ 야단치다 ☐ 시작하다

P174~175

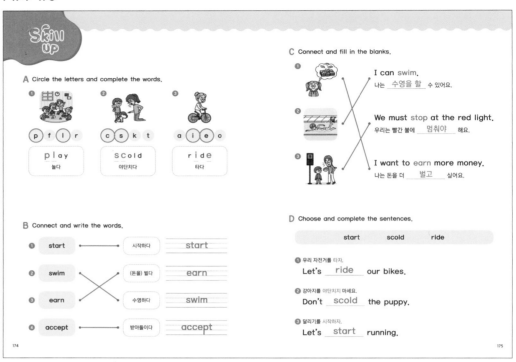

Skill UP

A Circle the letters and complete the words.

① p f l r → p l a y 놀다
② c s k t → S C o l d 야단치다
③ a i e o → r i d e 타다

B Connect and write the words.

① start — 시작하다 → start
② swim — (돈을) 벌다 → earn
③ earn — 수영하다 → swim
④ accept — 받아들이다 → accept

C Connect and fill in the blanks.

① I can swim.
나는 _수영을 할_ 수 있어요.

② We must stop at the red light.
우리는 빨간 불에 _멈춰야_ 해요.

③ I want to earn more money.
나는 돈을 더 _벌고_ 싶어요.

D Choose and complete the sentences.

start   scold   ride

① 우리 자전거를 타자.
Let's _ride_ our bikes.

② 강아지를 야단치지 마세요.
Don't _scold_ the puppy.

③ 달리기를 시작하자.
Let's _start_ running.

174   175

P176   P178

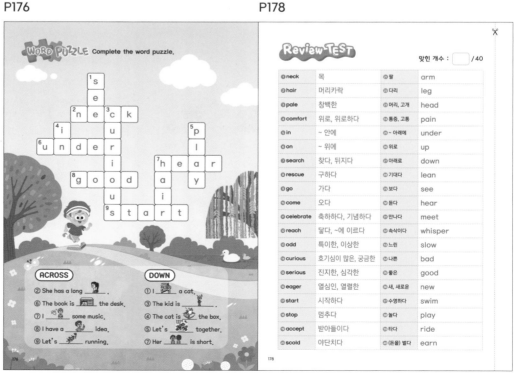

WORD PUZZLE Complete the word puzzle.

ACROSS
② She has a long _____.
⑥ The book is _____ the desk.
⑦ I _____ some music.
⑧ I have a _____ idea.
⑨ Let's _____ running.

DOWN
① I _____ a cat.
③ The kid is _____.
④ The cat is _____ the box.
⑤ Let's _____ together.
⑦ Her _____ is short.

Review TEST   맞힌 개수 : ☐ /40

①neck	목	㉑팔	arm
②hair	머리카락	㉒다리	leg
③pale	창백한	㉓머리, 고개	head
④comfort	위로, 위로하다	㉔통증, 고통	pain
⑤in	~ 안에	㉕~ 아래에	under
⑥on	~ 위에	㉖위로	up
⑦search	찾다, 뒤지다	㉗아래로	down
⑧rescue	구하다	㉘기대다	lean
⑨go	가다	㉙보다	see
⑩come	오다	㉚듣다	hear
⑪celebrate	축하하다, 기념하다	㉛만나다	meet
⑫reach	닿다, ~에 이르다	㉜속삭이다	whisper
⑬odd	특이한, 이상한	㉝느린	slow
⑭curious	호기심이 많은, 궁금한	㉞나쁜	bad
⑮serious	진지한, 심각한	㉟좋은	good
⑯eager	열심인, 열렬한	㊱새, 새로운	new
⑰start	시작하다	㊲수영하다	swim
⑱stop	멈추다	㊳놀다	play
⑲accept	받아들이다	㊴타다	ride
⑳scold	야단치다	㊵(돈을) 벌다	earn

176   178

Word List

a

accept	받아들이다
afraid	두려워하는
afternoon	오후
angry	화가 난
anxious	불안해하는, 걱정하는
argue	다투다, 언쟁하다
arm	팔
attach	붙이다
attack	공격하다

b

baby	아기
bad	나쁜
bare	맨, 벌거벗은
beach	해변
beam	광선, 빛줄기
beauty	아름다움
bed	침대
big	큰
bird	새
blanket	담요
blue	파란색(의)
bold	대담한
bottle	병
boy	남자아이
bread	빵
brother	남자 형제(형·오빠·남동생)
business	사업, 업무
button	단추, 단추를 잠그다

c

calendar	달력
call	부르다, 전화하다
cap	모자
carve	조각하다
cat	고양이
celebrate	축하하다, 기념하다
chair	의자
chew	씹다
clerk	점원, 직원
close	닫다
color	색깔

come	오다
comfort	위로, 위로하다
complain	불평하다
cook	요리사, 요리하다
cookie	쿠키
create	창작하다, 창조하다
curious	호기심이 많은, 궁금한
cute	귀여운

d

dad	아빠
dance	춤추다
dawn	새벽, 날이 밝다
desk	책상
doctor	의사
dog	개
down	아래로
duck	오리

e

eager	열심인, 열렬한
ear	귀
earn	(돈을) 벌다
edge	끝, 모서리
egg	달걀
empty	비어 있는, 빈
enemy	적
enormous	거대한
eraser	지우개
evening	저녁
exchange	교환하다
eye	눈

f

face	얼굴
fair	공평한, 공정한
family	가족
fast	빠르게, 빠른
fasten	매다, 고정시키다
fierce	사나운, 격렬한
fish	생선
flavor	맛
flower	꽃

follow	따라가다
food	음식
frown	눈살을 찌푸리다

g

gather	모이다
giraffe	기린
girl	여자아이
gloves	장갑
glue	풀
go	가다
good	좋은
grateful	감사하는, 고마워하는
green	초록색(의)

h

hair	머리카락
happy	행복한
head	머리, 고개
hear	듣다
honey	꿀
horse	말
host	주인, 주최하다

i

imagine	상상하다
in	~ 안에
insect	곤충
instrument	악기, 기구
item	물품, 품목

j

judge	판사, 심판

k

key	열쇠

l

label	라벨, 상표
lean	기대다
leg	다리
lion	사자
long	긴

m

man	남자
meat	고기
meet	만나다
milk	우유
mom	엄마
moon	달
morning	아침
mountain	산
mouth	입
move	옮기다, 움직이다

n

neck	목
nervous	불안해하는
new	새, 새로운
night	밤
noon	정오(낮 열두 시)
nose	코
nurse	간호사

o

object	물건, 사물
odd	특이한, 이상한
old	나이가 든, 낡은
on	~ 위에
open	열다

p

pain	통증, 고통
pale	창백한
peer	또래
pencil	연필
people	사람들
perform	공연하다, 수행하다
person	사람
plant	심다, 식물
play	놀다
polite	공손한
pretty	예쁜
protect	보호하다, 지키다

r

rabbit	토끼
reach	닿다, ~에 이르다
red	빨간색(의)
remove	벗다, 치우다
rescue	구하다
rice	밥, 쌀
ride	타다
ring	반지
river	강
room	방
rude	무례한, 버릇없는
run	달리다, 뛰다

s

sad	슬픈
scold	야단치다
search	찾다, 뒤지다
see	보다
serious	진지한, 심각한
sharp	날카로운
short	짧은
sick	아픈
silent	조용한
sing	노래하다
sister	여자 형제(누나·언니·여동생)
sit	앉다
sky	하늘
slow	느린
small	작은
smooth	매끄러운
soil	흙
spread	바르다, 펴다
stand	일어서다
star	별
stare	응시하다, 빤히 쳐다보다
start	시작하다
stop	멈추다
sun	해, 태양
surround	둘러싸다, 에워싸다
swim	수영하다
symbol	상징

t

tall	키가 큰
tape	테이프
teenage	십 대의
temperature	온도
tense	긴장한, 신경이 날카로운
tidy	깔끔한, 잘 정돈된
tie	넥타이
tiger	호랑이
tools	도구, 연장
tree	나무

u

under	~ 아래에
up	위로

v

various	다양한, 여러 가지의

w

walk	걷다
whisper	속삭이다
wind	바람
woman	여자
wrap	포장하다, 싸다

y

yellow	노란색(의)
young	어린, 젊은

z

zoo	동물원